Self-Publishing on KDP the Write Way

WITH JENNIFER HASKIN

TABLE OF CONTENTS

Note from the Author:

In writing this book, I tried to keep my regular teaching tone, discussing information I've said to many authors over emails, video classes, and Discord chats. I want you to feel like I am talking directly to you.

I can be passionate about things because this book is part of a system I've learned through grueling trial and effort. But I am happy to share it with those who need it.

If I am not clear about something or you need further explanation, please drop me a message so I can try to make it clearer—with an edit and/or a blog post.

Publishing really isn't scary once you learn more about it. It's a business, like anything else. Yet I truly empathize with new authors. It is frightening, and authors are kept in the dark. That's why I wrote this book and chose a conversational style.

I am by no means a #1 New York Times Bestseller ... yet. That is not the writing talent level I've grown to so far. But I know my system works—even for my humble fiction. You don't have to be able to run a marathon to teach others about the best ways to win—you need experience. And that, I have.

So take advantage of my hard-earned knowledge and publish your great book to rank well. I find the older a book gets—unless it is a favorite—it takes a few promotions here and there to stay relevant, but with a good book that is new, this system runs itself. My newest book outsells my first trilogy combined.

Lastly, I apologize to the paperback readers for the lack of color. It will appear in the ebook and hardback. With Amazon's cost raise, the color print price is high for readers, but I wanted that option to be available.

I really hope you find the answer in these pages to boost your book, whether a newly published book or an older one that wasn't ranking well. You can do it. And if you don't succeed, write a new book and try again. Good luck!

WELCOME

Hello! Welcome to my tutorial on self-publishing with KDP. My name is Jennifer Haskin, and in publishing, I was an agent first—about eight years ago—then became a consultant for almost a year before moving to where I am now, as Associate Editor at TouchPoint Press (a small publishing house). I am a professional editor for Reedsy and own my own publishing business. I am an author myself, first traditionally published, then indie. So, I understand how scary the unknown is and how confusing all this can be. But don't worry; I will help you understand it and know what to do.

I put together this course, an extensive class with a *lot* of information and the steps you need to take for your best chance at success. **As you read, please keep a notebook by your side and jot down any questions you have,** specific to your book or not. Hopefully, they will be answered in the text, but I always like to know where people need more information. I may include your suggestion in future editions or address it in a blog post.

First, we want to talk about the process of buying a book. The reader goes to Amazon, finds the bestseller list in their genre, and scrolls through thumbnails of book covers until they see one that catches their eye, then they stop and click. Next, they read the book's description. Now, **your description needs to seal the**

deal. They may look at other things on your page, like reviews and ranking, but if the description doesn't sell them, you've lost the sale.

Let me tell you my story, and you'll know why we are doing this. Years ago, I had an agent who got me a pretty dismal contract with a small publisher who turned out to be a man and wife team who published HER romance novels, and they thought, "Hey, let's do this for other authors and keep 60% of their money." (They wanted 90% on ebooks) So, I was published, and then, when the newness of the launch died, I slowly but steadily slid down the ranks until I was holding a bestseller ranking around the seven millions.

I remember thinking, "People aren't NOT buying my book based on the content. They don't even know what my book is about, because they don't know it's there." I believed that if they gave my book a chance, people may really like it. *So, how do I fix it?*

I took a year off and studied marketing. I learned that the higher-ranking books were seen more often and therefore clicked on more often, getting more sales that gave them a higher ranking that kept them at the top. It's a cycle. You are either cycling up or down. I learned that to raise my ranking and chances of being seen, I needed to know about *keywords, categories, descriptions,* and *covers*—the things we will discuss in this class. So, I figured it out and did all the work for my book. I researched my categories and keywords, wrote a new description, and got a new cover made. Then, I took all that to my publisher and said, "Here you go. Just type all this stuff in there for me, and we're good. I'll be selling in no time."

He said, "Technically, *I* own the book, not you. And if I thought any of that would make a difference, I would do it, but it's not going to make any difference, so I'm not wasting my time."

Well, at that point, I was convinced I had the answer, so I bought back my rights. We went around and around, then the publisher charged me $2,000 for my rights (because they can legally charge you any amount they choose), and my husband about had kittens. He said, "We're putting *more* money into this book that's not making any money?"

And I said, "Yes. Yes, we are."

So, I self-published my book on KDP instead of *them* publishing me on KDP (most small publishers use KDP for their clients' books, which means you lose royalty money to Amazon AND the publisher). I put in my new keywords and categories, added my new description and new cover, and low and behold, for the next five years, I ranked on the first two pages of my top three categories.

- **Best Sellers Rank:** #82,696 in Kindle Store (See Top 100 in Kindle Store)
    - #14 in Teen & Young Adult Dating & Intimacy eBooks
    - #30 in Teen & Young Adult Sci-Fi Action & Adventure eBooks
    - #31 in Teen & Young Adult Science Fiction & Dystopian Romance eBooks

We will learn all these things in this class. The first half of it is the most time-consuming but necessary to rank higher and be seen. It's all about exposure. You can't sell books if you're not seen. It's a numbers game. Have you heard that a person must see an ad seven times before they finally click on it?

In Amazon ads, it tells you how many times a person sees your ad (Impressions), how many times they click on it, and how many sales you make. It is said for every 1,000 impressions, you should get 100 clicks, and for every 10 clicks, you should get 1 sale. Now, that is a big "SUPPOSED TO." I generally don't hit those numbers, but there are some people who regularly exceed them. The point is, you need to rank in a place where many people are going to see your book many times.

I know it all sounds overwhelming, but I'm here to help. We'll go over everything together.

> *You need to have a dynamic cover that will make the reader stop scrolling and click on it, then a description that seals the deal, and a great book that gets good reviews.

Beware, there are programs that, for a fee, will "help" you self-publish. Let me be clear. Publishing should NEVER cost you a dime. The only things you should be paying for are editing and your cover. When publishing with a large OR small publisher, there is no cost, and there may even be an advance with the larger ones—but it shouldn't cost you. Self-publishing is also free. Now, there are people out there who will *assist* you, but the problem is that often you don't know what you don't know. Things may look great and professional, but you may not know what you're truly getting and what you're not. For example, one popular company that I saw charged an exorbitant amount to publish the author's work, but the steps involved in their process were generally unnecessary.

The site charges close to $4,000 for its "package." Though, when you read what is included in the package, you find: They have beta readers but *can't guarantee* a team member will be interested in your book. Editing comes with a separate charge. They run you through how to get an ISBN, barcode, and copyright from the Library of Congress but don't do it for you, plus there are charges there. (When you publish on Amazon, they will give you one for free.)

The company does no typing or content creation. The cover includes words and *one* stock image—anything else is an additional cost, and formatting is up to 280 pages of text only. Anything else costs more. The company also sets you up with a printer, but then you are required to buy a "print run" of 500 or more copies, and though you hope to sell that many copies, if you don't, or if you change the cover, the title, or re-edit, you will be stuck with boxes of paperbacks that you can't do anything with.

This is all for paperbacks, though. They do NOT even do ebooks. However, for an *extra* charge, they will give you a copy of your manuscript in ebook format. *We will learn in this class that it's not that hard to make your own.* Again, if you must end up publishing your ebook on KDP anyway, you can just as easily publish your paperback there as well, for free, and it's a print-on-demand system where Amazon only prints your paperback when one is ordered. So, no one has extra boxes of books lying around. Amazon does it all for you.

Don't be fooled by the enticement of "easiness" with these companies. It sounds like a dream not having to do any of it, or at least not market yourself. Right? They may offer to spam the internet with your book and get you all the publicity you need. They can put you on social media, just like I could, but unless they have a solid reader base, it won't be effective—especially if the company isn't well known. In this company's list, it says it gives the author a list of marketing "How-to's," but any *assistance* with marketing—you guessed it—costs extra.

There will always be people who are happy with their service—because they didn't have to do *some* things—but trust me when I say that marketing will always be your job as an author. Even in the Top 5 houses nowadays, with a marketing budget and a team, unless you are an established bestseller like Stephen King, you are still required to do a substantial portion of your own marketing work. There is no way around it. However, when you self-publish like we are going to do, **you have control of your book(s) and your information. You can change your cover or description on a whim if they aren't converting, and you can determine if your ads were successful or not.**

Other companies do formatting only—for about $250. They focus on desirable fonts, drop caps, and tiny flourishes, but all things you can do yourself for free. The benefit of this would be if you wanted an underlying image on certain pages; however, that can be done as well.

There are even companies that say they are "free" because there is no money *upfront*. But believe me, you will still pay for things you don't need and miss out on things you do need. But I am going to hold your hand through this process so that you are comfortable and knowledgeable.

> In short, these companies take advantage of your lack of knowledge and fear of the unknown to charge you for things that are pretty simple to do, and we're going to learn how to do them in this class to protect you so you don't get taken advantage of.

Why KDP?

Why are we publishing on Amazon KDP, specifically? Because Amazon is where readers go to find new books. Seventy percent of *all* book sales are made on Amazon. Amazon is easy to work with, offers assistance, and gives you access to sell on other platforms like Apple, Kobo, etc. Amazon reviews are the ones that count when adding up reviews for marketing, etc. When someone asks you how many reviews you have, they mean Amazon reviews. As a company, Amazon may not have the best moral compass, but you need them to sell books, and it's easiest to just start there.

With all that said, let's get started. We have a lot of information to cover, so remember to take notes that you will keep with your worksheets for the next book you publish. The worksheets (you will find them at the end of the course) will be your guide for future books until you know all this information by heart.

The Best Titles

"Don't judge a book by its cover." Although this sounds like great moral advice, it should not be taken literally. A great title and cover should capture your audience and convey the tone of your book. You should, with the book's title and cover, be able to tell what genre and age group the book belongs to. Is it a dark mystery? A sunny beach read? Is it an erotic romance or a sweet and wholesome romance? Those things should be clear between the title and cover.

For example, my first book was titled, *The Key of F*. It was about a magical key that a girl's father gave her before his death, calling it her destiny. First, Amazon kept putting my book with music books: the key of G, that sort of thing. I couldn't convince them I didn't belong there. Then, they figured out it was about a literal key, and they listed me with keyfobs, keychains, key-making, and home repair. See, nothing about *The Key of F* screams YA, fantasy, or romance. I ended up having to change my title three years later, which was a great pain, but at least from *Princess of the Blood Mages*, you get more of the feeling of a dark YA fantasy.

Your title should generate interest and intrigue without giving away too much of the plot. It should hook your audience with a little bit of plot and tone. Non-fiction titles explain what problem the reader has that the book can solve. It's a different game in attracting readers. (Non-fiction books will still use this system, and it's easier to sell non-fiction books, so if that's you, read on.)

> Take some time to think of titles you know and jot down what you feel makes them work or what makes them appealing.

Traits that good titles have in common:

1] **They are short.** This makes them easier to remember.

2] **They are compelling.** These titles are evocative. Use your writing skills to convey imagery. I love it when the title is sewn into the book, or you get ¾ of the way through the book, and the title suddenly makes sense. It's an "aha" moment.

3] **They are unique.** Whenever I get a title idea, I go to Amazon to see who already has my title or how I might need to tweak my title to fit yet be unique.

4] **They are memorable.** Either by the literary methods you use or something the title identifies, something about the title makes it easy to remember.

5] **They clearly show genre and age group.** Amazon considers your title and subtitle when deciding where to place your book in front of readers, and you want to be in front of the *right* readers.

There's a different set of vocabulary that is used in genre titles. Romantic books may call for dreamy language. Thrillers may have either vague words with a spooky cover or specific words featured in horror books. Action books would have strong, powerful words. Show the feel and tone of the subject matter. Let the reader feel the action or drama, or impending doom. As soon as you can grab the reader—go for it.

> Your goal: Get the reader, keep the reader.

In choosing your title, there are many ways to go about it and many concepts available to use:

--Compare other best-selling titles. You do want a title *similar* to others in your genre so the reader knows what kind of book you have. Lately, YA fantasy titles have been "A something of something and something." *A Battle of Sun and Sand, A Castle of Ash and Gold, A Sword of Silver and Death.* That sort of thing. So, if you had a YA fantasy, you would want to go along with that trend. (I'll explain more in a bit.)

--Character names or character qualities that draw emotion. Think of *Charlotte's Web.*

TITLES USING CHARACTER NAMES

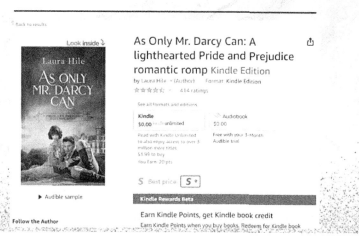

--The antagonist's name or position may be a good title if the story revolves around them. Sinister-sounding names give a feeling of dread. Think: *Hook* (as in Captain Hook)

--Who impacts the story most? Like the first two, who is the story *really* about? Could the focus character be someone who is not the protagonist or the antagonist? Think: *My Sister's Keeper* (if the keeper was not the protagonist)

> Sidenote: People want a book that makes them *feel*. That's why we read. We want to be emotionally invested, involved in a story; we want to be able to feel as if we are there with them.

--Where and when the setting takes place can give us a clue for our title. Think: *Love in the Time of Cholera*

--Alliteration or double entendre are tools you can use. Alliteration is the occurrence of the same letter or sound at the beginning of adjacent or closely connected words and also the repetition of an initial consonant sound, as in "a peck of pickled peppers." Think of *Gone Girl*. (Double Entendre is a word or phrase that is open to two interpretations, one of which is usually risqué or indecent. Maybe a book about a rebuilt car named *Hot Body*?)

Examples:
Pride and Prejudice
The Great Gatsby
Sense and Sensibility
Of Mice and Men
The Two Towers
A Christmas Carol
Peter Pan
Black Beauty
Wind in the Willows

War of the Worlds
The Prince and the Pauper
Love's Labor's Lost
Gone Girl
East of Eden
Angela's Ashes

--You can also use book generator tools. Try these: Create Your Own Story Title Generator, Story Toolz Half Title Generator, etc. I like to use these to brainstorm. You can enter your genre and get words that are popular within it. As much as we want to be separate and totally unique, remember, you **want** to go with your genre's trends.

The reason is this: Say the reader goes to their favorite genre's page on Amazon with the top fifty books, and all the popular ones have the same sound and/or look in common. The reader has already read the top-sellers and enjoyed them, then they come across your book, and it looks similar, and the title is on-trend, and they think, "Oh look, there's one of those books I like!" *That* is why, as much as it sounds great to be original, at some point, you want to be clicked on. You just want to have readers. And to win that click, you've got to look and sound like the other great books in your genre.

--For non-fiction, write down the problem that you're solving. Tell the reader they have a problem (maybe one they didn't know about) and how to solve it. Again, make it memorable. Use alliteration or whatever literary tools that fit. Add character to your book and attract readers.

Play with the title, tease the reader, intrigue them, and cause them to remember your book—and to click on it. You want them to think, "I've got to read that!" Pique their interest. What parts of your story are captivating? What emotions do you want your title to convey? Do you want them to shiver? Do you want them to laugh? Do you want them to smile? What feeling do you want to evoke?

Choose a theme and come up with five or so titles that pull on different parts of that.

What if your book is a romance and your theme is not a car but a guy with a really hot body? Your title can play off that with puns (*Better a hot body, than a lukewarm personality*), play on words (*Hot body, cool mind*), like phrases (*She's hot-headed, he has a hot body*), or the title could be the theme itself: *Hot Bodies*.

There's something to be said about shocker titles. As long as you aren't listed in "Home Repair" like I was. (Lol.) Any way you can stop the reader from scrolling long enough to be intrigued and click on your book, you must try it. The people who know what title will fit your book best are the ones who would pick it out of a stack—your audience. That's why it's so important to know who your audience is. Not only do you write to them, but you want to get feedback from your target audience. Sometimes they are elusive. Young adults, for example, can be hard to track down on social media as they hide from adults whenever possible.

In that case, ask a writing group. Or take a poll on social media. Given choices, most people are happy to weigh in on a quick poll. Ask family and friends, only those **who already read your genre**.

When asking friends and family, never take them something like your title and description and ask them, "Is this good?"

First of all, they don't know what you're going for and often can't put their finger on the advice in writers' terms to tell you what to keep or what to change. Plus, Gramma's never going to say, "No." She may say, "Oh, it's great, honey. You might do this or that..." But you are not going to get an unbiased opinion. Gramma just can't do it.

What I suggest is to take three to five versions of what you are trying to do and ask them, "Which of these descriptions makes you want to know more? Which title produces an emotional reaction in you?"

Not, "Is this good," or "does this work?" If it's all you have, it's what's working. Give choices to get a variety of feedback.

TIPS FOR GETTING GOOD FEEDBACK:

FACEBOOK:
- CREATE A POLL IN A FACEBOOK WRITING GROUP

FRIENDS AND FAMILY
- REACH OUT TO SOME FRIENDS OR FAMILY YOU KNOW WHO READ YOUR GENRE AND ASK FOR THEIR FEEDBACK

TWITTER
- POST A POLL ON TWITTER WITH YOUR VARIOUS OPTIONS

- DO ALL OF THESE IN ORDER TO GET A WIDE VARIETY OF INPUT

One of my clients had a book he'd titled *Head Voice*. Can you guess what its genre and age group are? Take a second and think about it. In my last class, people guessed "psycho-thriller," "street gang memoir," and "self-help book." *Head Voice* is actually a young adult novel about a teenage boy who cheats his way into a fancy boys' choir to go on a trip to Italy and sing for the Pope. Before he leaves, he meets a girl who, by a whole different route, takes a vacation romp through Italy, and they end up meeting each other there in Rome and fall in "like," then he sings to her at the end. The author and I brainstormed, and we threw a bunch of words around and ended up with *Madcap Serenade*.

Would you ever have guessed that *Head Voice* would be a young adult boys' choir, romantic Roman adventure? *No.* Nobody else would, either. But *Madcap Serenade* lends itself better to a zany trip to Italy with music involved. It gives a better tone to the story. You expect with a name like "madcap" that there will be exciting adventures.

> The point is, you need to know, "What am I conveying/ not conveying with my title?"

Subtitle Options

Non-fiction books use subtitles to convey the problem they are solving. The title lists the problem, and the subtitle tells us how to fix it. When deciding on your non-fiction subtitle, consider:

- How can your subtitle expand on the need and solution of your issue?
- What are the biggest problems in your book that the subtitle can show how to solve?
- How else can you advise workable solutions that would be helpful to people with the problem you are discussing?

Examples of some explanatory subtitles:

- Sleeping Problems With Your Infant Or Toddler? Struggle No More!: *A Parenting Guide With Simple & Proven Strategies To Implement For You & Your Baby To ... Struggle No More*
- Saving Ourselves from Suicide—Before and After: *How to Ask for Help, Recognize Warning Signs, and Navigate Grief*

- Expect to Manifest Your Best Life: *Activating the Law of Positive Expectation (Metaphysical Self-Help Book 1)*
- Letting Go Of Friends: *How To Recognize & Deal With Toxic Female Relationships (Non-Fiction, How To Make Good Friends)*
- Rain: *A Dark Romance Age Gap Love Triangle*
- Beyond the Crushing Waves: *A gripping, emotional page-turner*

The subtitle should give extra ideas, fill in the blanks, or make the title clear: *Help Me, I'm Stuck* could mean anything, but its subtitle makes the title clear: *Six Proven Methods to Shift Your Mindset From Self-Sabotage to Self-Improvement* (The Help Me Series)

In fiction, certainly in YA, authors have begun to use their age group and genre (or tropes) as their subtitles. For example:

- As The Secrets Turn: *Romantic Suspense Stand-alone* (My Darkest Secret Book 3)
- Mark of the Fool 2: *A Progression Fantasy Epic*
- Curse of Shadows and Thorns: *A Dark Fairy Tale Romance* (The Broken Kingdoms Book 1)
- The Divine and the Cursed: *A Fae Fantasy Romance*

Things to remember: The subtitle is not the series title. You don't have to have the subtitle you enter into KDP printed on your book. If you already have a subtitle on your book cover, use that. In KDP, there is also a space to put your series name, and Amazon will give you a "Series Page" for all the books in your series if you enter the information during the upload. But don't confuse subtitles with series names.

My subtitle says: *YA fantasy romance*. And the reason you want to do this is that Amazon uses keywords to know where to place your book in front of readers, and it gets those keywords from your title, subtitle, and description. Tropes can be genres and keywords as well.

Having your age group/genre as your subtitle lets your readers know if this is a book they are interested in; it puts you in niche categories and is helpful as far as your ranking goes. And so far, it works really well.

TITLES WITH GENRE SUBTITLES

HITCHED: A DARK HITCHHIKER ROMANCE

ASK FOR ANDREA: A TENSE AND GRIPPING THRILLER WITH AN UNFORGETTABLE ENDING

FLOWERS FOR THE DEVIL: A DARK VICTORIAN ROMANCE

RULE NUMBER FIVE: A COLLEGE HOCKEY ROMANCE

ONE BOSSY DATE: AN ENEMIES TO LOVERS ROMANCE

ONE MOMENT PLEASE: A SURPRISE PREGNANCY STANDALONE

MARK OF THE FOOL: A PROGRESSION FANTASY EPIC

A DRAGON'S CHAINS: AN EPIC FANTASY SAGA

ALONE: A PARANORMAL MYSTERY THRILLER

TITAN MAGE: A HAREM FANTASY ADVENTURE

Descriptions That Sell

The book cover attracts the readers' attention, and the title intrigues them, so they click (Yay!), and now *your description* has to seal the deal. The description decides if you get the sale.

Take some extra time on this. Look at other descriptions. Some people are going to call your description your "blurb," and some will call it a "description." Some even call it a "synopsis." It doesn't matter. But for our purposes, it's the sales description you have on Amazon that is meant to entice readers to buy your book. It is NOT necessarily the back cover copy.

Unless you are in brick-and-mortar stores, the people reading the back cover of your book have probably already purchased it, so it doesn't have to be super catchy. Though, you can create and use your best description as a modified version on your back cover if you wish. That's fine, too. I find with the description on Amazon, most people never even read the back cover online.

Here's the thing: Make it interesting. Hook the reader into saying, "I have 5,003 books in my TBR, but I need to read this one right now!" Use keywords so Amazon knows where to show your book.

Amazon says in ***How to write your book description,*** "We recommend following these three simple steps for writing an

24

effective book description. Make it simple, compelling, and professional."

Describe the main plot, theme, or idea only. Avoid details that may overwhelm or confuse a reader who's only taking a second or two to decide whether to find out more about your book. Also, keep your language short and simple. Aim for 150-word paragraphs with sentences that are easy to scan. Scanability is important in a description.

I know some people who see two big blocks of text and think, "That's too many words," and skip it altogether. (Then, you've lost the sale.) But that's because it's too many words in a row. If you break it up into smaller paragraphs, it looks easier to read. Make it four or five smaller paragraphs not to look overwhelming.

Avoiding overwhelming and confusing details will help make your description compelling, but also consider how to grab readers' attention. For example, write a first sentence that draws them in. This sentence may be a reader's first impression, so make it special. Also, set expectations by showing what genre your book belongs to. The first sentence in your description needs to be what we call your "movie poster" line.

You know, the guy in the movie trailer that says in a super deep voice, "In a world of danger and intrigue, two archeologists face the evil of the mountain in the only way they know how—with his wits and her trusty ancient sword of doom…"

My book says, "He wants to rule the world. She was born to stop him." And another one says, "**The winner will be crowned Ambassador's Bride. The losers will meet certain death.**" It's a line that makes you want to say, *dum dum dum* after it. It could be a question. "Can Katy overcome all the forces against her since her accident?" It's designed to make the reader want to know more. *How does he want to rule the world? Who's dying? What happened to Katy, and how will she overcome it?* Create questions in the mind of the reader.

PROFESSIONAL

Again, this might be your reader's first impression, so make sure your description is polished—no misspellings or grammatical errors. When you see a mistake in the description of another author, do you lose a bit of respect? My mother learned English as a second language when she was a teenager. And when she learned it, she learned all the details, where commas go, punctuation, grammar, all of it. The stuff we piddled through in 8th grade English and hoped we'd never be tested on again? She knows it. And if she sees an error in the description, she is going to think, "Well, there are probably mistakes in the book, too." *Right?*

> If you don't take the care needed for this little description, how do they know you took enough care in your manuscript? You must earn the trust of your readers. It may be hard to edit a piece of text you've looked at several times, so show it to others to get a fresh set of eyes.

BREAKING IT DOWN

Brian Cohen runs a class through his business called the "Amazon Ad School." He runs it several times a year, and it is free, but you need to register for it. (Here's a year-round link for Author Ad School -https://bryancohen.lpages.co/author-ad-school-enroll-now) The link is for his school program. Get on his mailing list for the free class. Brian teaches authors how to make Amazon ads and how to use the information Amazon gives you to test your ads and make better ones. He suggests a formula for writing your description (though he calls it a blurb).

Sales copy formula ala Brian Cohen (This is for your sales description on Amazon):

1. Headline/hook phrase (movie poster line) *dum dum dum*.

2. Synopsis (what it's about)

3. Selling paragraph (their emotional benefit—why they would want to read this)

4. Call to action—*One-click now! Grab your copy today!* Something that directs the reader to respond in the way you want.

DESCRIPTIONS

1. HEADLINE/HOOK PHRASE (MOVIE POSTER LINE)
2. SYNOPSIS (WHAT IT'S ABOUT)
3. SELLING PARAGRAPH (THEIR EMOTIONAL BENEFIT)
4. CALL TO ACTION (BUY NOW!)

Let's start at the beginning:

~1. First, make up your movie poster line—that one/two phrase synopsis meant to hook the reader into reading the rest of the description. (Know your conflicts and consequences.) This will take a while. Make a few options to run by your friends and family. Which one makes them want to click? Which is most effective? Which one makes them want to know more?

~2. Then write the synopsis portion. Let's break that down.

For the first paragraph:

Sentence 1. Your protagonist's state of being—how their world is now. *Suzie is a young girl who never knew who her parents were and was raised by a horrible woman and her daughters. She lives in the shadows, bowing to their every whim. At night, she fixes mechanical devices for her household and others, secreting away the sparse money she makes to one day get away.* (Build toward the inciting incident.)

Sentence 2. Tell us the inciting incident to the midpoint. *One day Suzie comes home, and her room has been ransacked, her money stolen, and her machines destroyed. Her adopted mother stands sneering with a willow rod in her hand and says, "You have only done this to yourself, Suzie." After a brutal punishment, her mother says if Suzie ever betrays her again, she will beat her within an inch of her life and lock her in the basement for the next five years.* (Bum bum bum.) *Suzie is distraught and in pain from the punishment of her mother discovering all her secrets and stealing her meager savings. But as she sits outside sobbing, the kindly mailman hands her a flyer for a mechanic's contest that would pay her way out of town forever.* (Now, her life is going to change.)

Sentence 3. How the inciting incident or midpoint impacts your character emotionally [Don't just summarize the plot; tell us how it impacts the characters.] *Suzie is tortured by the idea of remaining there. Her fear of her mother propels her through days of work and nights of preparation for the contest. She has two exhausting weeks to be ready. Suzie must take outside orders fixing machines to pay for a ticket into the big city, risking exposure every night. She makes many mistakes but doesn't give up.* (We have a purpose now. Or this could be the part where the mystery of the story becomes known.)

Second paragraph:

Sentence 1. Character's new state of being [in the heat of the story]. *She huddles in a carriage house, clutching her paper with shaking hands, afraid to leave and more afraid to stay. She is terrified of being found by her mother or having her mother send a man for her.*

Sentence 2. Build up to the conflict/cliffhanger (what they want & what's in their way) *Frozen in fear, she wonders if she will be good enough to win the prize because if she doesn't, she will have no choice but to go home and be punished, forced into the basement, or live in the city's dirty streets and starve or freeze to death. She momentarily turns back.*

Third paragraph:

Hint at how Acts 3 and 4 will impact the characters emotionally. *Suzie's entrance to the big city is full of excitement as she marvels at all the gears and mechanical items she's never seen before. How will she know how to fix anything here? She can't possibly win. Will her mother find her—come to drag her home? Suzie keeps an eye on everyone she sees, fearful of being knocked on the head by a hired man and being pulled back home. She never wants to go there again. She meets a young contest judge who offers to give her the winning score in exchange for a risky favor. If Suzie accepts, she could be caught and thrown in jail. If she doesn't accept, she will lose when the judge lies to the other judges.* (What are the stakes? –The stakes in a book are: *what will happen if the good guy loses?* Is the world at stake? Will they lose their life, liberty, or one true love?— Provoke a response in your readers. End this portion with the highest stakes. The whole point is to HOOK the reader, so tell them what the dire consequences are and leave them wondering what will happen and feeling a need to find out.)

~3. Write the selling paragraph:

What is it, and why will I like it? *This coming-of-age romance thrives on danger in a perilous plot for Suzie. If you like heists with a twist and dark, dangerous societies, this is for you.* (This is where you say, "If you like xyz, then you'll love this book!" Use comp books here. *For fans of such and such*, or *readers who love blank book meets blank book…* This is also called a "high concept." (When the plot is easily explained in a simple sentence) My fourth book is also a high-concept book. It is "The Selection meets the Hunger Games in space." I took two of the best-selling books in my genre and asked myself *what would happen if these two were mashed together?* It's a great way to choose a new plot. Ask yourself, "What if?")

~4. Call to action:

What should the reader do now? *Buy now!* or *One-click to start the adventure!* (Etc.)

KEYWORDS

FOR ROMANCE, USE WORDS LIKE:

FAST-PACED ADVENTURE,
ENEMIES TO LOVERS,
COMING OF AGE,
COZY MYSTERY,
CLEAN AND WHOLESOME ROMANCE,
DARK DANGEROUS SOCIETIES,
STRONG FEMALE LEAD,
ADOPTION,
HATE TO LOVE,
BEST FRIEND ROMANCE,
HOT CRUSH,
GROWING ATTRACTION, ROMANCE BLOOMS…

Use keywords in your description like *Fast-paced adventure, enemies to lovers romance, coming of age, cozy mystery, dystopian future, clean and wholesome romance, dark and dangerous societies, strong female lead, adoption, hate to love, twisted mystery, best friend romance, romantic suspense, hot crush, growing attraction, romance blooms…* Anything that you can think of that a reader of your genre might type into the search bar that might bring up your book.

All those keywords help Amazon place your book, and the better you're placed, the more relevant readers see your book. *Exposure.* See, when the reader goes to their favorite genre's bestseller page and starts at #1 on page one, they scan until they find the cover that catches their eye. If it's in the first row of five books, *they're done.* No more looking; *they've found a book to read.*

(I don't necessarily like to shop that way. I'm a window shopper. I like to know if there's another one I'll like better.) But for a *lot* of people, if you are anywhere but the first page, your chances of getting clicked on just get slimmer and slimmer. So, follow all these directions. It's not as hard as it sounds, but it is a little time-consuming.

Don't worry about the keywords at first; just write a good description, then go back and see where some good keywords might fit or where you might exchange a phrase for a keyword phrase. Maybe instead of an adventure, it's a *fast-paced adventure*, or not just a cute guy but a *hot crush?* But there is more on that to come in *Keywords*.

Your description must be engaging. It must provoke a response in readers. Ask for help if you need it. Ask your writer friends. Of course your friends will like it, but does it make them want to read the book? I can't stress this enough, come up with 2 or 3 versions of your description and ask people in writer groups online for their opinions. But do NOT ask, "Is this good?" or "Do you like this?" ASK, "Which one of these makes you want to buy the book?"

Same as with friends and family. They don't know what you're shooting for, and they want to encourage you and make you happy, so of course they liked it, of course they think it's good, but does it make them want to *buy it?* Does it pique their interest? Does it tell them enough about the story to make them want to read it but not so much that they think they already know the whole plot? Leave off the ending. *Does dowdy Jane have a snowball's chance in hell at attracting Tom, the CEO of a big company?* You know she will because that's what the book is about, but you have no idea *how* she's going to do it. Make the readers have questions. They will want to read to find out the answers.

I also like to use Kindlepreneur's book description generator (see below). You write your description in the box, then you can make your heading bigger, and you can do bold, italics, bullet points, etc. If there are bullet points (usually for non-fiction), Amazon uses the first 100 characters after a bullet point as keywords. So, I have, at the end of my description, a few tropes that are keywords after bullet points. And Amazon uses the keywords to know where to place my book.

The Description Generator formats your text into HTML format and easily uploads to your KDP Detail page for publishing. It's very helpful for formatting your description. And as a new function, you can use Kindlepreneur's AI to help you write a better description.

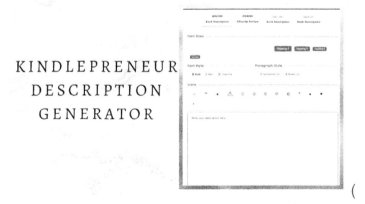

KINDLEPRENEUR
DESCRIPTION
GENERATOR

(https://haskinauthor--rocket.thrivecart.com/publisher-rocket/5da9eaeda2e47/)

Finding Profitable Keywords

You will enter **seven keyword phrases** when you upload your book to KDP and fill in the details, and you will select your **three categories**. Do your research *ahead of time* and find marketable keywords for your book. Amazon looks for keywords in your description to know where to show your book (There's a science to it. So it would behoove you to have someone write you an engaging description if yours isn't selling. Pay for it if you have to. It's the difference between making sales or not).

Now, when I say keyword phrases for KDP, I'm not just talking about trope words or words that you think go well with your genre. They specifically want **phrases that a reader would type into the search bar when looking for a book like yours**. They are very close to your other keywords, but a subtle difference that again changes the algorithms, and they are generally a string of at least two or three words.

The best way to discover these keyword phrases is to go to Amazon (and I would do this in "incognito mode" so that Amazon isn't taking your preferences into account), and in the search bar, begin to enter words that you think a reader might enter for your age group and/or genre. The age group only matters for Children's books, Middle Grade, or Young Adult. If it isn't specified, it is assumed to be for adults. Now, make sure where it says "All" to the left of the search bar that you have clicked on "Kindle Store" as your place to search. As you type into the search bar, Amazon will show a drop-down menu with the most popular searched keyword phrases.

For example, let's look at a couple. When I type in "middle grade," the list gives me ten of the highest searched phrases. There is *middle grade mystery, middle grade chapter books, middle grade fantasy*, and *middle grade books for girls 9-12*. That last one is pretty specific. If your book falls under one of these keywords, then that is a good keyword for you to use. But you don't need an age group specifier if your keywords are something like "coming of age." You want to type slowly and see if the list changes with each letter you add. If you enter "coming" and a keyword pops up that matches your book, jot it down. Not all readers type in the whole word or phrase. If they type "coming" and their option pops up, they just click on it from the menu.

Let's try it. I typed in "coming" and at the bottom of the list was *coming of age fantasy*. If that's you, jot it down. "Coming o" brought up *coming of age, coming of age fantasy, coming of age fiction*, and *coming of age romance*. I'll keep going though… "Coming of" only added *coming of age science fiction* to the list. "Coming of a" kept what we had and added some interesting options like *coming of age in Samoa, coming of age sports fiction football,* and *coming of age in Mississippi.* Okay, getting more specific. "Coming of ag" and "coming of age" didn't add anything new to the list.

You are going to do this with every phrase you can think of that a reader might type to look for your book. Now, how do you guess these phrases? You can look at other comparable (comp) books and see what they have as their subtitles and keywords that might pertain to your book, you can take a shot in the dark and guess the phrases used, use a keyword generator, or you can use a tool that does it all for you, such as Dave Chesson's Publisher Rocket Tool. Here is a link to it: https://haskinauthor--rocket.thrivecart.com/publisher-rocket/.

This tool (for now) has a one-time charge ($97) with lifetime access. I highly suggest it, especially if you are going to self-publish. This tool can help you find keywords, categories, Amazon Ads keywords, and comp books. It gives you information on your competition, THEIR keywords, and categories, as well as their daily and monthly sales. I can't tell you how important that can be when you are wondering, "How did they get there?" or "What are they using?"

Amazon has complicated algorithms that change often, and Rocket changes with them in real-time, as all its info is current. In fact, the software itself updates to better serve you, the author, three times a day and also frequently upgrades, free of charge. They have reliable and fast tech-support if you have a problem. It shows you categories that Amazon itself does not list, helping you discover information you could have never found otherwise. It lists book and/or ebook categories, as authors may not realize they are different. And Rocket now includes audiobook information as well.

This is what Kindlepreneur says about the tool: "*Publisher Rocket helps authors identify the most profitable keywords for your book. How does it do this? It analyzes the top five books that use that keyword based on certain criteria. First, you type in a keyword into the keyword search bar and then hit 'Go Get Em Rocket.'*

Rocket analyzes the top 5 books that use that keyword based on the following criteria:

1. *Book popularity*

2. *Fame and strength of the authors*

3. *Age of the books*

4. *# of reviews and review grades*

5. *Whether or not the keyword is in the title/subtitle*

6. *Enrolled in Kindle Unlimited or not*

This is a key feature of the Rocket software.

It tells authors:

- *How many people are typing in that keyword/phrase*

- *Competition score of that keyword from 1-100.*

- *How much money the top 5 books are earning on average*

- *# of competitors using that keyword*

Without this data, you wouldn't be able to figure out how many people are using this keyword or if it is being searched for at all. The keyword feature eliminates the guesswork and provides accurate data.

For a complete walkthrough of how to use this feature, Publisher Rocket has an easy-to-follow tutorial: **Keyword Search Feature of Publisher Rocket**

There are tutorials on just about anything you want to do.

- **Publisher Rocket pays for itself:** *There are three ways that you users will earn back the initial investment spent on PR.*

- *The cost of Rocket is $97.00. If the Rocket saves you 5 hours of your time, you just earned back your money. How much is your time worth per hour?*

- *When you sell about 47 books priced at $2.99 (at 70% royalty) because you could find profitable keywords and better categories, the software just paid for itself.*

- *If Rocket helps you to filter out a bad book idea because nobody is searching for it and gets you to change your marketing efforts based on proven data, it definitely just paid for itself. This will save you thousands of dollars and hundreds of working hours you would have spent on a book that won't sell.*

- ***Gives authors a competitive edge.*** *You can access the most up-to-date data on categories, keywords, and AMS ads. You can also figure out the best kind of books to write before you write them so you don't publish something nobody wants to buy. This is a big win for an author who has the goal to write for a living and wants to make real money in self-publishing. And you can analyze the competition as we have seen, to stay ahead of the game and get your books out in front of readers first."*

Let's give it a try. Say we have a **Middle-Grade feel-good book about a boy and his bird**. We can look in Publisher Rocket for different things. First, if we look (on the next slide) at the Category Search, we can see that in the category *Kindle ebooks> Children's ebooks> Animals> Birds*, most of the books are indie and are also on Kindle Unlimited. You would only need to sell 11 copies to be #10 on the ranking scale, but you'd need to sell 81 copies to be #1. So, it is a competitive market.

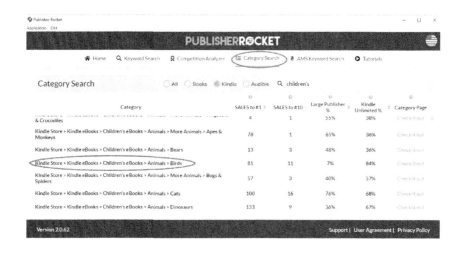

If we take a look at the competition with the Competition Analyzer below, we can see the books that we will be competing with. We can see the titles and covers, the *categories* they are in, *how old* they are (age), their *bestseller ranking (ABSR)*, *number of pages*, if they used *keywords in their title (KWT)*, what *price* they are selling for, then *daily sales (DY)*, and *monthly sales (MO)*. You can also click "check it out" to see its sales page. This is useful information to have on your comp books. It helps you know where you stand in the rankings and what you need to do better.

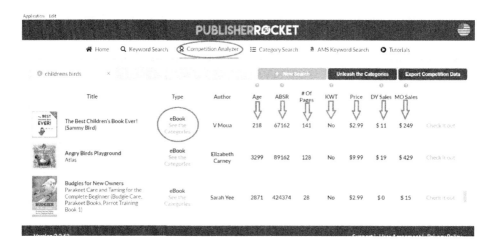

Finally, let's take a look at some keywords. I typed in *Children's books about birds*. You can type in any keywords you choose and keep pulling up new searches until you have what you need. For this one, the only keywords it brought up that fit us are *children's books about birds, children's books about animals, children's books about emotions,* and *children's books about feelings and emotions.* So those are the only ones I will click on (click the orange magnifying glass on the right, and it will turn into a green square). That keeps the info pertinent to me and is less confusing.

Below we can see *how many people we are competing against*, their books' *average price, how much they make per month*, and *how many times that keyword is searched for each month*. So, the first one, *Children's books about birds*, is searched for 688 times a month. That's not bad, and there are fewer than 1,200 competitors, so this is a good keyword. And the competitive score at the end confirms this with a green 40. The next entry, however, is searched for 2,062 times a month and has less than 1,200 competitors, which seems like a dream, but the competitive ranking shows a red 80. So why is that?

That's because the keyword, *children's books about animals*, is too vague. The reason it is searched 2,062 times is that the searcher may be looking for birds, or horses, or pigs, or all animals, or farm or jungle animals. The chances that they are going to click on books about birds with this keyword phrase are extremely low. So, this is not a good keyword for you. And the red 80 lets you know that.

Keyword	Average Pages	Number Of Competitors	Average Price	Average Monthly Earnings	Est. Amazon Searches/Month	Competitive Score	
childrens books about birds	72	>1,200	$12	$2,883	688	40	
childrens books about animals	147	>1,200	$14	$4,055	2,062	80	
childrens books about cats	-	-	-	-	-	-	
childrens books about diversity	-	-	-	-	-	-	
childrens books about emotions	60	>1,200	$19	$21,331	6,357	85	
childrens books about feelings and emotions	45	>1,200	$12	$18,128	629	85	
childrens books about food	-	-	-	-	-	-	

Once you get all these keywords or competitors pulled up, do you have to write all this down? Nope. There is an option to "Export," and all your new keywords and information can be downloaded into an Excel spreadsheet to use as you need.

Again, here is the link to the Publisher Rocket Tool— https://haskinauthor--rocket.thrivecart.com/publisher-rocket/ (This is an affiliate link that won't change your purchase, but gets me a pat on the head.)

Another is a tool called *Keyword Tool,* and you can find it here: www.keywordtool.io. It does something similar. You put in your keyword, and they rank on trend and search volume. It works better for using ads because it tells you what your competition is bidding per click.

www.WebFX.com also has a keyword suggestion tool. You must register with your email first.

The online free tools also target products in their searches, not just books, as KDP Rocket does. Rocket might bring up a few products if your keyword doesn't produce much, but it generally lists books exclusively.

Now, you can do this legwork yourself (and in this class, I show you how), but if you have Publisher Rocket, the work has been done for you. All you need to do is work with the tool. Moving on…

CHOOSING THE RIGHT CATEGORIES

We learned how to use Amazon's search bar to find relative keyword phrases and how to use KDP Rocket, but how does a self-publishing author find the right categories on their own? Keep reading.

*Up till now (and not everyone knew this), you could actually be listed in up to **ten** categories!* No joke. I was recently listed in thirteen without knowing it, but I have gone back to ten or eleven. There was nothing scammy or dishonest about this. That way, you could be broad in some categories and very niche in others and see where you ranked the best. I don't know if that will change for books that already have ten categories or not.

There is a new change coming into effect this summer (2023) where the author will only be listed in **three categories**. Period. It used to be that Amazon would automatically list you in one category, and then you entered two basic categories of your own. However, the categories they had listed for authors to choose from inside KDP were called BISAC categories, NOT their regular categories. Once your book was live, you could log onto www.AuthorCentral.com with your Amazon password (This is where you will claim your book and manage your platform. More to come…) and request to add the rest of your categories.

But now, KDP will be listing regular Amazon categories in KDP, including niche categories, and authors will choose the three that they will be listed in. That makes this even more important to get right. You need to know them *before* publishing. Find your category and subcategories to get the one you want. Then, click the button below (not shown) that says "Add another category" to reset the choices. When you are done, it will look similar to this:

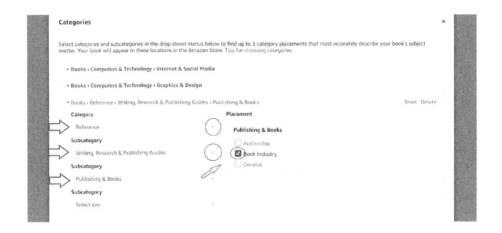

This will take some prep work. I suggest going down the list of categories on Amazon and writing down *every one* that your book would fit in. You will notice that some of the categories are doubled or found in a different, less obvious way. These "niche" categories are smaller and not as competitive—giving you a better chance to rank higher in them. And the higher your rank, the easier it is to be seen by readers. Never forget EXPOSURE is the word.

To find your categories, you are going to go back to Amazon, and from the white menu bar, you can choose either *Kindle ebooks, Kindle Unlimited, Kindle Books, Kindle Vella*, etc. I choose *Kindle ebooks* because that's where I sell more. But it's not a bad idea to choose one or two "Book" categories for hard copies, as well.

Once you click on Kindle ebooks, there is a menu on the left side. (If it doesn't appear, try clicking on the main (blue) menu where it says Bestsellers.)

You will have to scroll down the menu on the left to where it says: Kindle Store and click on it. Now your menu looks like this:

Click on *Kindle ebooks* in the menu (Circled in red). The categories listed are adult categories. If you are in YA, scroll down to *Teen & Young Adult* and click there first. If you are in Children's or Middle Grade, click on *Children's eBooks*. Now, you are going to go down the list of categories and click each one. Yes, this sounds like a lot, but it ends up being fun to do.

If you click on any listed genre, you'll see another whole list of subcategories appear under it. You are going to click on these as well. That will give you the niche categories. For example, if you have a Scifi Romance, you can click on *Kindle ebooks> Science Fiction & Fantasy> Science Fiction>* and a list pops up with more options, but there is no romance option, so you'd choose the other options that might fit your book, maybe *dystopian* or *space opera*.

Then you would go back to *Kindle ebooks* and click on *Romance*. If you click *Kindle ebooks>*, then *Romance>*, "*Science Fiction*" comes up as one of your options. That would be a niche category (Not a category that many would expect a science fiction book to be). I hope that makes sense.

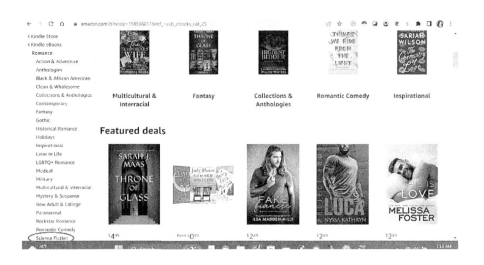

Let's do another one. Say you have a Mystery, ala Sherlock Holmes that is dark and has some thrills. We can't do them all, but some of your options could be:

Kindle ebooks> then *Mystery, Thriller & Suspense>* Your remaining list says: 1] *Crime Fiction*, 2] *Mystery*, 3] *Science Fiction*, 4] *Suspense*, 5] *Thrillers*. (See below) Ours could be any one of these, so let's check them out.

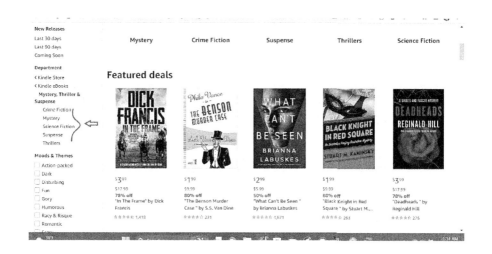

1] For *Kindle ebooks> Mystery, Thriller & Suspense>* try *Crime Fiction*. Now, under this one, we get a whole new menu of niche categories that says: *Heist, Kidnapping, Murder, Noir, Organized Crime, Serial killers, Vigilante Justice*. Clicking on each of these shows that they are each the end of the thread, so choose any that fit the book. We are going to choose 1] *Kindle ebooks> Mystery, Thriller & Suspense> Murder,* and 2] *Kindle ebooks> Mystery, Thriller & Suspense> Serial Killers* for our book.

2] Let's go back to our list *Kindle ebooks> Mystery, Thriller & Suspense> Mystery,* that's the end of the thread, but you will notice Amazon's list has changed to put you in *Kindle ebooks> Science Fiction & Fantasy> Science Fiction> Mystery*. That must

45

be a niche way to get there, and it is an alternative category option for you. So, the first one might be the main category, and the second one a niche category. Write them both down.

Keep going down the line with 3] *Science Fiction*, 4] *Suspense*, and 5] *Thrillers*. Then go back to *Kindle ebooks* and look for the next category. Look at categories that even loosely connect to your genre. I suggest clicking them all because often, you will find a niche category that matches you in another category you never would have guessed. And those are great finds.

If your book is a *coming of age* romance in the *young adult* category, you may also choose to put it in the *adult romance> coming of age* category as well.

NICHE RANKING

WHERE YOUR YA DYSTOPIAN BOOK MIGHT RANK LOW IN:
KINDLE EBOOKS> TEEN & YOUNG ADULT> SCIFI & FANTASY> SCIFI> DYSTOPIAN

YOU MAY RANK REALLY HIGH IN:
KINDLE EBOOKS> TEEN & YOUNG ADULT> ROMANCE> SCIFI & DYSTOPIAN

The main point of doing all the clicking is to find categories that match your book and making sure you find ALL the categories that match your book. So, where your YA dystopian book might rank low in:

Kindle ebooks> Teen & Young adult> Scifi & Fantasy> Scifi> Dystopian

You may rank really high in:

Kindle ebooks> Teen & Young adult> Romance> Scifi & Dystopian

That's because the second category string is a niche category. I didn't go straight to *Scifi* as the big category. I went through *Romance*. Now, if there's not a drop of romance in your YA dystopian, I'll have to check you for a pulse, but in that case, you wouldn't want to go through romance for the niche category because it would frustrate people if they got the book thinking it's one thing and find it's another. So, stay true to your book, but don't just go for the obvious categories first.

*Note: Kindle eBook categories are NOT the same as print "Book" categories. The categories may be different or absent and will not rank the same. So, if you want your paperback to do as well as your ebook, make sure to research your categories thoroughly. This means you will probably have different categories for your kindle ebook and paperback copies.

When we get to uploading our manuscript, we will choose the three best categories from your list. You can see how using Publisher Rocket makes this easier to do and easier to find which categories you've found that are best for you.

Updated news [10/8/23]—Dave Chesson from Kindlepreneur recently put out a new article regarding the category change and you may be alarmed. Read on. Out of your choices of categories on KDP, 54% of the categories are duplicates and 27% are "ghost" categories.

An example of a duplicate category follows:

Books> Mystery, Thriller & Suspense> Mystery> Historical

Books> Literature & Fiction> Historical fiction> Mysteries

Books> Literature & Fiction> Genre Fiction> Historical> Mysteries

Being in one of the above categories means that you are seen in all three category chains, but they all end up in the same place. This could be beneficial. One category they found had over fifteen duplicates!

Ghost category pages just say *Bestseller* at the top and don't have the category title or the category tree to the left. You cannot get a bestseller tag in these categories and readers can't look them up.

Lastly, Amazon states in their TOS and on their FAQ pages that they have the right to "change your categories" from the ones you selected and/or add additional categories. They choose your categories by considering 1] the selections you made, 2] the keywords you used, 3] your description, and 4] your book's content. So, choose categories that fit well and consider using category-specific words with your keywords. If the categories fit your book really well, it may encourage Amazon to put you in a few additional categories of the same type.

So far, there is a long way to manually look for duplicates, but it is problematic as most duplicates are in different strings. And I can't figure out how to tell which categories are ghost categories, without looking up each one separately. The good news is that Publisher Rocket will now tell you with each category if it is a duplicate and/or if it is a ghost category. Another great reason to invest in this tool.

Sometimes a category that you are doing well in, suddenly gets popular, and all of a sudden, you aren't ranking well anymore. This is a great time to go back to Rocket and re-check your categories. Just select the new ones on your Details page (more on that coming) and make sure to hit "publish" to make changes final—if you have published already.

[Updated News 11/2/23]—I have a disturbing issue regarding categories. I was ranking on the first page of two of my chosen categories and the third page for my third category. So, I thought I would optimize, and I used Publisher Rocket to find categories where I would be on the first page (that match my book, of course) and changed my categories. But now I am only ranking in ONE of them. One of the others fits loosely, and the third category I'm ranking in does not fit my book at all. I am neither a *paranormal* nor an *urban fantasy*. I have gone round and round with Amazon, trying to get them to rank me in my three chosen categories. But apparently, they don't work that way anymore.

First, I found this in the new category information:

"After you choose categories for your book, we recommend limiting changes to allow time for your book to gain momentum with readers. If you frequently change your categories, historical customer activity for your book may be recalculated based on your new categories, which could impact your sales rank.

Boy, does it ever.

I talked to many people in customer service who kept telling me that my ranking had to do with something else:

"Customer activity influences which three categories your book can be ranked in as a best seller. Your book's detail page will display the top three category rankings only. This explains why the categories you add in your book's Details tab, and the three showing on your book's detail page may not match."

I was still unsatisfied, thinking I was not listed in my chosen categories. and I filled out a customer service survey, saying that I wasn't happy with the service, and told them my issue again. I received an email saying that they confirmed I AM listed in those categories; however, I am not ranked in them. I don't know how I am IN a category without RANKING in it. But this is what they said:

> *"While you are able to choose the categories that you would like your book to be available in, your book will also rank in categories different to these.*
>
> *These rankings are based on what a customer was searching for, on the Amazon website, when happening across your book. This does not mean that your book is present in these categories per se, but rather that, when the customer initially searched for something appealing to them, their search eventually, based on their click-throughs, led them to your book, and they then chose to either make a purchase, or click on your book to learn more about it.*
>
> *Unfortunately, since we cannot foresee what a customer will search for when purchasing books, or foresee which customer behaviors will cause them to choose your book in particular, we do not have control over your sales rank. It is purely based on sales, as well as how the Amazon search algorithm connects your book to certain keywords.*
>
> *The keywords are a combination of what you selected during Title Setup, as well as internal Search Engine Optimization models, and search attributes.*
>
> *While your sales rank categories cannot be modified, I would like to be clear about the fact that these categories are not assigned to your book, even though they are currently ranking there.*
>
> *It is based on external factors, and they are subject to change, according to consumer behavior at the time of purchase, or click-through."*

I wrote them back, telling them I was upset. It doesn't make any sense to ask authors what categories they want if they don't rank you in any of them. Unfortunately, in not ranking my book in my categories, they have halted my organic sales. I put my book on sale to see if new purchases would change my ranking, as they should. But apparently, since people clicked the links from my ads, I was not "searched" for on Amazon, and therefore, even though

I made twenty-four $0.99 sales in the last week, my ranking didn't change at all.

I am at a loss. I don't know how to fix this. I went from ranking on the first page, to ranking #800 in a category that doesn't match my book at all. This is going to be a problem for more authors. It seems that when you first put in your categories, it works the way it should. But if you change them before Amazon has had a chance to confirm your sales with those categories, they will refigure your rank based on customer searches. So, CAREFULLY choose your categories the first time, and then *don't change them!*

What Cover Do I Want?

M any people solidly versed in cover design—and I am by no means one of them—will tell you NOT to put a scene from your book on the cover. And others will tell you to absolutely use a scene from the book. You will hear varying amounts of advice about covers, but I'm going to be very honest here and give you my best advice. This won't be too long because the answer is: you want your cover to look like the bestselling covers in your genre.

YOU WANT YOUR COVER TO LOOK LIKE THE BEST-SELLING COVERS IN YOUR GENRE.

You may have heard that before, but *what does it mean?* That was something I always used to ask.

I will share the secret right here with an example. When I wrote my first book, I went with an "original" cover, and no one clicked on it. Oh, I launched well and then slowly slid down Amazon's list, ranking in the seven millions. The readers weren't NOT reading my book based on the content. They didn't know what it was about because they weren't clicking on it.

So how did I get a "clickable" cover? I learned. I learned a lot from people on the net who know their stuff and share their knowledge. As you may know, I write in the Young Adult age group and the fantasy, sci-fi, and romance genres. At that time—about five or so years ago—young adult fantasy covers had either a girl in a pretty dress or an up-close face. *See the photo.* (It has changed since then, so don't rely on that now.) So, I chose a better cover in the style of the bestsellers, and when the style changed, I changed my covers again. I don't rank too high in the YA fantasy *general* category since it is so saturated, but since you could have up to ten categories, I ranked high enough in a few of them to keep me in the ranks and selling. I am no longer in the seven millions and unknown.

THESE COVERS ALL HAVE THE "GIRL IN A PRETTY DRESS" IN COMMON

So, what you do is go to Amazon, click *Bestsellers,* and then click through the left-hand menu until you get to *Kindle ebooks*, then find your genre. When you click on it, the books that appear are your genre category's top fifty bestsellers. Notice the similarities of the books on the first one or two pages. What do they have in common? Do they have people or symbols? Do they have scrolly designs? Are the backgrounds blurred or clear? Are they light or dark? If you have a mystery, do most of them have a dark background, with a splash of color and a man's silhouette with a building behind him? You can see it in your mind, and you know what kind of book you're going to get when you see a cover like that. Are the covers mostly illustrated or photos? Do they have faces on them or whole bodies? Are the fonts similar? Is the cover text blocky or script? Serif or not? Pay attention to the things these first fifty to one hundred books have in common.

THAT is what you want on your cover.

I hear you. I said the same things. "But I don't want a cookie-cutter cover. I don't want to look exactly like someone else's cover. Besides, that's not original. I want to be original and stand out from the crowd."

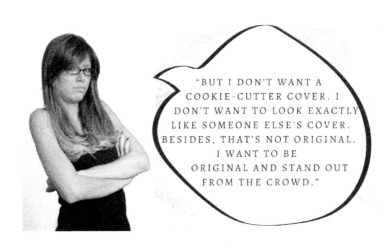

Great. You do that. And all the bestseller-similar covers in your genre will continue getting more clicks. Why? Their covers. Here's why, when the customer comes along and sees a cover like one of the bestsellers that they **already love**, something in their brain says, "Oh look! There's one of those books I like." Remember? Then they click on it to read the description. That's *exactly* what you want.

If they don't love your cover, they don't click, so they don't read your description, and they don't buy. It is really that simple. And smart authors keep an eye on the trends, so when their comp books from the top publishers change to some new design that *they* all have in common, you change with them. Then readers who come across your book think, "Oh, look…!"

Once you have the *right* cover, your assignment is to get all the exposure you can for your book. I continue to do that by running Amazon ads. I run them for the US, UK, Canada, Germany, Spain, and Australian Amazon markets. Right now, 83% of my sales are in the UK, but that fluctuates. Some months they don't know I'm alive, and the US market picks up. I started bidding really low, like $0.09 per click, but I wasn't getting seen, so through trial and error, I raised the price up to about $0.21-0.31 per click. It is worth it if you've added good comp books and authors as your keywords and your cover matches theirs. Then, when a reader looks for that book or author, your ad shows up on their page. That gets a lot of exposure, but you have to remember that for every 1,000 impressions, you might get anywhere from 10 to 1,000 clicks, and you will hopefully get 1 sale per every 10 clicks.

So, you NEED a lot of exposure to get all those impressions (that's when a customer sees your book) to get the clicks you need. Then it's up to the reader if they like your description enough to read the book.

And that's it. Simple but a little time-consuming. I have paid upwards of $800 for one cover, and I've made some myself. It's sometimes a crap shoot. I understand. I feel pretty good about my ability to choose covers now, but it's taken five years of learning. The point is, start learning now, and you'll get there. Most new authors have grand expectations for their book, and there's nothing wrong with that, but many of us who were with a small publisher or indie realize relatively quickly that without a big marketing department and/or budget, books fall down the scale.

If you take what I've said to heart and give it a try, I believe you will *sell more books*. One last reason to know what your cover should look like is when hiring a cover designer. When you hire someone to design your cover, they will ask what you want on it. Then they will give you exactly what you asked for. If you don't know what type of cover and what attributes you need to make a selling cover, then neither will your designer.

Don't go to Fiverr for a cover; look around. You can have someone on Fiverr write your description but NOT to make your cover. For your description, you'll want to pay someone about $25 to get something worth your money. You can also find online coupons for $100 off at 100covers.com (covers for $100 and up), and they will let you make changes so you get what you want. They hire professional artists, but you should know if what they make you is the right cover—or not. Don't say it's fine if it isn't.

If you have three books in a series, their covers need to be similar to each other. It's called "branding." With a series, they must go together. If Penguin Random House and Macmillan all change their covers to match, and you decide to follow the trend, you want to change the covers to all three books in your trilogy. While you're writing the series, keep your brand matching, but when it's done, you have the option to change them along with the trade books.

You can also make a cover with the KDP cover tool. You can even make one that says, "coming soon" if you are going to be on preorder. Then when you get your final cover, you can have a "cover reveal." You can poll your fans or have whatever fun you want with that.

TITLE FONT/AUTHOR NAME FONT/TEXT COLORS

Notice the fonts used on the type of cover you are leaning toward. Are they in specific colors or color combinations? Get fancy with your title font but leave your author name smaller and in a sans-serif font. (Sans serif font doesn't have "serifs" on the letters—the little line at the bottoms or tops of letters. For example: "Serif F" and "Sans serif F")

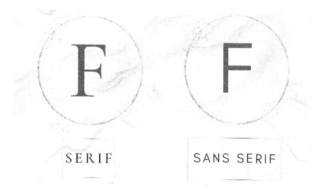

SERIF   SANS SERIF

Formatting the Book

If you have the first chapter of the next book ready, especially indies, I suggest you **add it to the back matter** of your book. Those authors who do, see a 20% increase in sales for the following book.

Back matter would be your *Acknowledgements, About the Author page, Other books by this author*, plus an excerpt from an upcoming work. The *front matter* would be your *Title page, Copyright page, Dedication, Maps*, and *Table of Contents*.

FRONT MATTER	• DEDICATION, • MAPS, • TABLE OF CONTENTS
BACK MATTER	• ACKNOWLEDGEMENTS, • ABOUT THE AUTHOR, • ALSO BY THIS AUTHOR, • AN EXCERPT FROM AN UPCOMING WORK.

Your covers will also need appropriate formats. The cover image you upload will appear on your Amazon sales page. You can choose to upload your own cover image, or you can use their free cover tool: https.kdp.amazon.com/help/topic/g201113520 to design a cover for your Kindle eBook and/or Paperback.

Your cover file must be a jpeg (image file). If you've made cover art yourself, you can use your Paint program to insert the picture, then scale to the following dimensions for the ebook: 1800 x 2700 pixels—300dpi.

The paperback cover size depends on how many pages your book has. (I can help with cover formatting, as well.)

Normally, I teach the formatting part over Zoom, so if you have any problems with your formatting, please let me know or schedule a one-on-one visit with me to go over this in detail. There is a worksheet for formatting your manuscript in your "worksheet package" that you can reuse with each book as you wish, and it is on page two of the worksheets at the end of this book. However, I will put it here (on the following page) and add any info I can. Of course, if you don't know where the formatting buttons are in Word to make the formatting changes, they are all on the ribbon at the top of the screen, but you can easily use Google to find answers to those questions.

E- Book Manuscript Formatting

Right now, I'd like to tell you what you can do *while writing* that will make your formatting easier. First, your font should be *Times New Roman, 12 point*. That may be the default choice with Word, so in that case, just don't change the font, and you're good. The default paper size in Word is *8.5 x 11"*, and margins are *1" on all sides*, which is what you want for your ebook, so stick with the default size and margins. Make your first page the title page with your title and name only. Leave your cursor there, and on the ribbon at the top, go to the *Insert* tab, and click **Page Break**. At the end of every chapter, click *Page Break* to start at the top of the next page.

Once you have typed a paragraph or two of Chapter 1, go to the *Home* tab and click the *Editing* box, then *Select*, then **Select All**. While your text is highlighted, stay on the *Home* tab and look in the *Paragraph* section. You will see this:

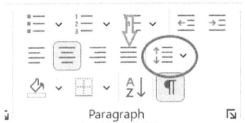

Paragraph Click this button and choose single spacing (1.15), and at the bottom of the list, make sure it says *ADD space before paragraph* and *ADD space after paragraph* (you may have to click it again). If it says, *Remove space* on either of those, then click it. Also, click to have the text *Justified* (where the green arrow is).

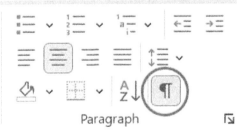

Paragraph Next, with your text still highlighted, go back to that section, and click this button to show your paragraph marks. This will help you to see your page breaks and your spacing (one space between words and after each sentence). To turn it off, just click it again.

Then, still highlighted, click the little box in the lower right corner.

This will bring up a new menu that looks like this:

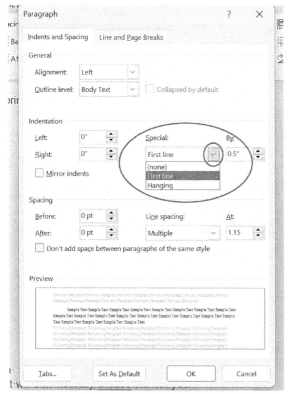

In the middle section, where it says *Special*, click the arrow and choose **First line**. It will automatically choose 0.5" for you. Click **OK** at the bottom. Now, your paragraphs will automatically indent for you as you type. If, for some reason, you hit *Enter* and the next paragraph does NOT indent, highlight the area, go back to this box, and click it again.

61

NEVER hit the tab button to indent your book. This is the way to do it.

You may choose to insert page numbers while you're writing to know where you are, but you will have to remove them before publishing. Ebooks scroll at a different pace than 8.5 x 11" pages, so if you have headers or page numbers in the ebook, they will seem to appear at random in the text, sometimes in the middle of a sentence, and it's very annoying for readers. But your formatting sheet will remind you to remove them.

Now, you are ready to get back to writing. It will be easier for you because the paragraphs will indent automatically, you can see your formatting, and there's no more pressing *Enter* a thousand times to get to the end of a page for the next chapter. Just click *Page Break* and keep going. Half of your formatting will already be done when you finish writing. But, if you haven't done these things yet, go back and complete the instructions. If you have pressed tab to indent or entered extra lines, you will have to remove them to format properly. It's best to start your formatting as you write.

Now, let's finish formatting the ebook. Here is a copy of the formatting worksheet checklist (To see better, go to *Part 2* in the section titled "WORKSHEETS," on pg.125):

Part Two: Formatting the Book
Ebook formatting checklist: Using Word (Can use Kindle Create) *Macs are different
Font: Times New Roman, 12 point
Make sure **first line** is indented to 5mm
Line spacing: single --No extra lines between paragraphs
Margins are 1" all around (this is the default- so you shouldn't have to change anything)
For each chapter title, highlight and click **Heading 1** on **Home** menu,
Add front matter--title page 1, copyright 2, dedication 3--Center on page
Insert table of contents after dedication page(Go to *References* page, click **Table of Contents**, choose table)
Add back matter--acknowledgments, about the author bio, also by the author
Add page breaks--at the end of each chapter, place your cursor at end of text and click on **Insert** tab,
then click **Page Break** (Click to show **paragraph marks** to make this easier)
No page numbers, headers, or footers
You may upload the file in Word, Epub, or from Kindle Create
Paperback formatting checklist:
Font: Times New Roman, 12 point, single spacing, no lines between paragraphs
Set **Page Size** to 6" x 9" (Some have their paperback 5.5x8 and their hardback 6x9, it's your choice)

Set Margins:	Page count	Inside (gutter) margins	Outside margins (top, bottom, and edge)
	24 to 150 pages	0.375 in (9.6 mm)	at least 0.375 in (9.6 mm)
*Go to Layout tab, under *page setup*, go to *margins* tab, *pages*,	151 to 300 pages	0.5 in (12.7 mm)	at least 0.375 in (9.6 mm)
multiple pages, and click "mirror margins," then add your other	301 to 500 pages	0.625 in (15.9 mm)	at least 0.375 in (9.6 mm)
margins and apply to "whole document."	501 to 700 pages	0.75 in (19.1 mm)	at least 0.375 in (9.6 mm)
	701 to 828 pages	0.875 in (22.3 mm)	at least 0.375 in (9.6 mm)

For each chapter title, highlight and click **Heading 1** on **Home** menu,
Add **Section** breaks--at the end of each chapter, place your cursor at end of text and click on **Layout** tab,
then click **Breaks**, then click **Next Page** (This goes everywhere your ebook had *Page Breaks*)
Add front matter--title page 1, copyright 2, dedication 3--Center on page
Add back matter--acknowledgments, about the author bio, also by the author
Click **Insert** tab, then click **Page Numbers**, choose *bottom* and *center* of page
Optional: Headers--Click **Insert** tab, click **Header**, choose style and type "Title/Author's last name"
Insert table of contents after dedication page
You may need to insert extra blank pages in the beginning to make sure Chap 1 starts on a **facing** page
Export as a PDF file--click on **File** tab, click **Export**, click **Create PDF** --Upload pdf file to KDP

As you can see, the first four items on your checklist will already be done if you follow my directions while you type. You just need to add your *copyright*, *dedication*, and *table of contents* pages to the front (front matter) and your *acknowledgments*, *about the author*, and *also by the author* pages to the end (back matter).

You can Google "copyright page" examples to choose what you want yours to say. Copyright goes on the back of the title page.

You will need to format every chapter heading (and that includes the titles for your front and back matter). In the ribbon, on the *Home* tab, in the *Styles* box, find where it says **Heading 1**. To format your chapter headings, first, **right-click** on *Heading 1*, then click **Modify**. From the box that pops up, format what you want your chapter headings to look like. Choose options from the box to design the font, color, spacing, center or left justified, and size. Then, when you go to the beginning of a chapter, type the heading you want and leave your cursor there, or go to the beginning of any heading, and click on **Heading 1**, and it will format it for you. If you *modify* the heading again, it will change all the headings automatically.

When you insert a *Table of Contents* (from the References tab), it will bring up everything in *Heading 1* format and put it with a page number. In your ebook, this will make all your headings into links, so you have a clickable table. Make your *Table of Contents* page right after your dedication page. You will want a Page Break after each **page** of your front and back matter, but only after every **chapter** in the text.

After that, your ebook is done. It is formatted and ready to upload (We will go into that in detail coming up). If you have the free **Calibre** app (https://calibre-ebook.com/download_windows), you can convert your Word file into an epub file to upload. This is what I use.

℘APERBACK ℳANUSCRIPT ℱORMATTING

The paperback formatting is a bit more involved, so I wait until I have the ebook ***completely*** edited and formatted, and ready to go beforehand. *Then* I make a copy of the ebook to format as my paperback because you will need most of that ebook formatting in place.

First, you will need to go to the *Layout* tab, click *Size*, click *More paper sizes*, then enter your new page size. While you are in that window, click the tab that says *Margins* to enter your margins. I generally have the *top margin* at 0.8 (to leave room for the header), the *bottom margin* at 0.7 (to leave room for the page number), and the *inside* and *outside margins* 0.4. If you have 100 pages or more, you'll want to click on **mirror margins**, and then I make my *gutter margin* 0.4 as well, so your words don't get lost in the crease of the spine. (Without mirror margins, you do not want a gutter margin) Your window will look like this:

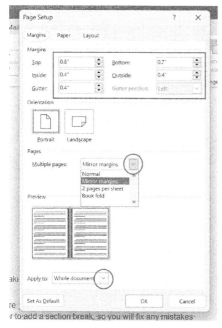

Make sure it says **Whole document** at the bottom. Click *OK*.

This, of course, will change where your chapter endings are, but no bother, you will need to go to the end of every chapter to add a section break, so you will fix any mistakes then. Everywhere you have a "page break" for the ebook, you will need a "section break" for the paperback. (Since it is not important to the ebook, but it is required in the paperback, some authors choose to end their ebook chapters with a section break, so it's already done here.) To do that, go to the *Layout* tab, click where it says *Breaks*, then click **Next Page**. You can delete the *page breaks* if you wish, but in my books, I have simply added the section breaks before, and that was fine.

You will add back in your page numbers (bottom, center of page) and add a header if you want one (title/author's last name). If you're feeling really zippy, you can put your last name in one header and your title on the opposite page's header. It looks professional, and I do it, but it is usually painful as not all pages take the hint and have to be fixed manually. I learned how to do this through good ol' Google, myself.

You want Chapter One to begin on a facing page. If you hold a book open, the facing page is on the right. It is not the back of a page. You may need to add a blank page to the end of your front matter to make sure your Chapter begins on a facing page, and that's fine. You don't have to worry about it for the other chapters.

On your *Table of Contents* page, which you still have from your ebook, you will go to the page and click on the **Table of Contents**. A box will appear like this:

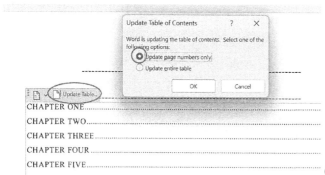

Click where it says *Update Table,* and this little box appears. Click **Update page numbers only**. That will make sure the new page numbers are correct.

If you have copied your formatted ebook, you don't have to worry about the front matter and back matter, except to make sure everything fits the way you want it to with the paperback file. You are done formatting. Click on the *File* tab, click on *Export*, then click **Create PDF**. And now, it is ready to upload into KDP. Let's move on to the uploading!

Uploading Your Ebook to KDP

This is an exhaustive look at KDP and the whole upload process, including every step (with screenshots). I am demonstrating with either a dummy account I use for teaching or my own book account.

1] Online, you will want to go to: www.KDP.amazon.com and click the "sign in" button. Use your existing Amazon.com password.

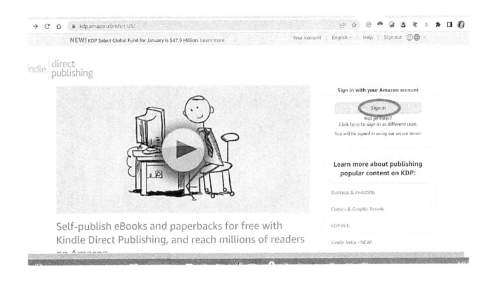

KDP opens to your Bookshelf (dashboard). Here is what that looks like:

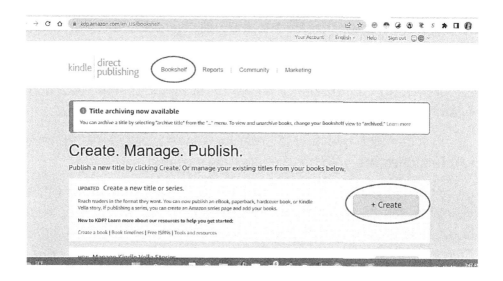

You will click the +*Create* button the first time you set up a book on KDP. Once you have established books, they will be listed on your bookshelf like this:

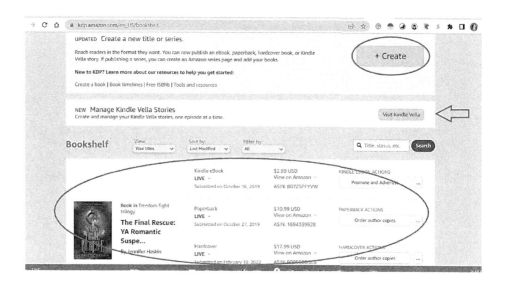

You can see by this book entry that the Kindle, paperback, and hardback versions are listed, along with their prices, their ASIN, their publishing status (LIVE), the book's cover, title, and subtitle, and "action" buttons to the right for each version. When you are finished and your book is live, the buttons say "Promote and Advertise" for the ebook and "Order author copies" for the paperback and hardback. Don't worry about these now; this is an example of what your dashboard will show you in the future.

You can also see how to enter the Kindle Vella store, which is where stories are sold by episodes (See arrow).

You can tell by this next book that it is in draft form with a yellow button that says, "Continue setup." Once you upload your book, unless you publish it right away, it will say *Continue setup*. This is the button you will push to continue your upload. After you've finished uploading your ebook, which I always do first, KDP will prompt you to make your paperback version. If you don't follow the prompt, you can see that there are buttons here that say "+Create paperback" and "+Create hardback" so you can use those in the dashboard if you wish.

KDP has three pages included in the upload process: *Details, Content*, and *Pricing*. If you click the yellow button to continue your setup, you will automatically go to the first page, *Details*. Or you can click the three dots on the button to its right, and a menu appears like this (below). From here, you can click to go directly to the page you need without having to click through them.

This is also the place where you can link or unlink the various versions of your book or add it to a series if you haven't already. You shouldn't need that option, though. We will cover that on the *Details* page.

At the top of the next page, you can see the three pages for uploading. You can also see a menu bar above that with *Bookshelf, Reports, Community*, and *Marketing*. We will go over each of these after uploading our book. (The worksheets at the end also have a checklist for uploading.)

1] Let's begin. Select your ***language***.

2] Add your ***book title*** and ***subtitle*** in the appropriate boxes. Under the subtitle box, you will see a button for series information.

71

3] **Author name**—put your name or your pen name, whomever you write as. Amazon will still know it's you.

4] Add **contributors**. This would be a co-author, or a children's book illustrator, etc. This is NOT for your cover artist. Anyone you list here will have a link to your book as a contributing author. Most of the time, it is left blank.

5] Add your **description**. You may use HTML-formatted content. I like to use Kindlepreneur's Description Generator and copy/paste the formatted description here. Don't slap something together. The reader needs to see your cover and stop scrolling and click it, but then your description is necessary for the sale. If you get them to your page and don't capture them with your description, you've lost the reader. Hire someone on Fiverr if you have to. (You'll need to spend about $25 to get a decent one.)

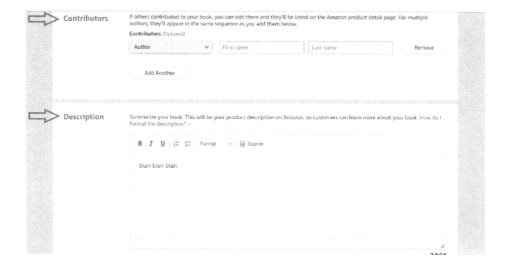

6] Below that, click "I own the *copyright*…"

7] Then add your seven **keyword phrases**. This is particularly important for determining where KDP places your book to be seen by readers. Think of short phrases that a reader might type into Amazon when searching for a book like yours. i.e. *YA fantasy romance, books for teen girls 13-16, epic sci-fi, mysteries for adults, books for the beach,* etc.

8] Next is ***Categories***. (The categories listed in the illustration are now the same categories on Amazon, not the old BISAC ones.) When you click on "set categories" a new menu will pop up. You will be able to choose three categories, and they will include niche categories. But if you've done the work, it's easy.

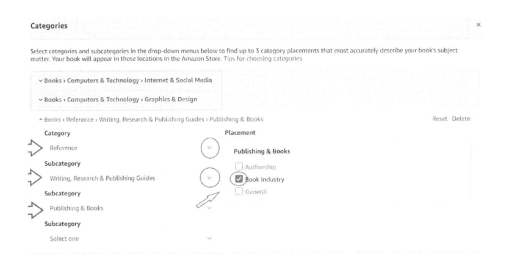

9] ***Age grade and range***. If you have an adult book, you don't need to worry about this, but if you have a Children's book, Middle Grade, or Young Adult, you must specify an age and grade range for your readers. You will run into difficulty if you do not. Click the "Select" buttons and then click the corresponding numbers.

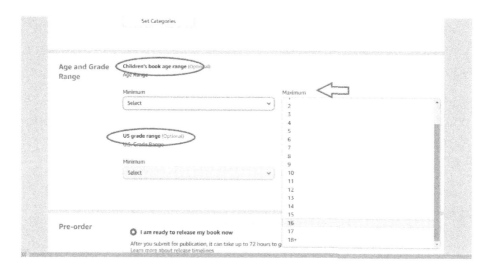

10] For the last item on the *Details* page, decide if you want to **publish** when you finish uploading, save it for later, or if you want to put your book on ***preorder***. You can be in preorder for up to a year. However, your book sales are NOT saved up for launch like they used to be. Amazon will judge your book sales from the beginning of the preorder period. So, you don't want to muddle through the preorder and then have a big launch because, to Amazon, it will look like a fluke sale. You want slow and steady sales to show Amazon that you are relevant and in demand.

So, either push your whole preorder hard with marketing from the start or skip the preorder. People appreciate having the product when they purchase it, so I recommend skipping the preorder and preparing to launch to a wide platform. Excite your social media in the weeks before launch. (I have a book coming with a section on launching.)

If you click "I am ready to release my book now," you can still enter your information and save it as a draft for as long as needed. So, if you are not going on preorder, click *I am ready to release my book now*. Then, at the end of the third page, click to *save as draft* rather than *publish*. You can continue to work on the three pages and save the draft until you are ready to click *publish*. Once you click preorder, set a date, and click "publish" on the third page, your date is set.

At the bottom, you will need to either *"save as draft"* to continue uploading at a later time or click ***"Save and Continue"*** to move to the next page.

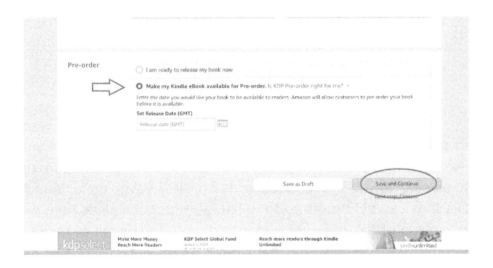

11] Now that all the details are taken care of, it's time to upload our content. On the *Content* page, click **DRM** to keep people from unauthorized distribution of your material.

12] Then, click ***"Upload ebook manuscript"*** and upload your formatted ebook. (There will be a page at the end of the book with instructions on how to format your manuscript.) Note that KDP wants a table of contents for each version of the book.

(After publishing, if you re-edit your book or make changes to it, come back to this page and upload your new version here. As soon as you click *publish* again, the changes will go into effect. So, you must "republish" every time you want to change keywords, your description, your cover, etc.)

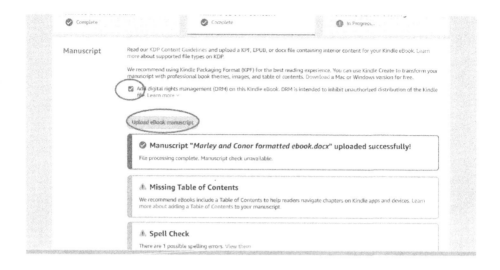

13] Scroll down and ***upload your cover***. You can either use *Kindle Create* to make a cover or *upload a jpg file* you've prepared already. We will take a look at the cover creator in the next images. (14] When finished uploading a new manuscript file and/or a new cover file, always click the button to ***launch the previewer***.)

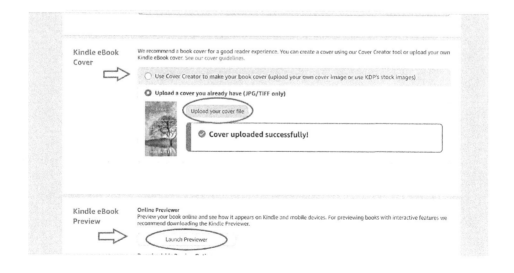

The following images illustrate how to use Kindle Cover Creator. After clicking the bubble, this menu pops up. Follow the instructions.

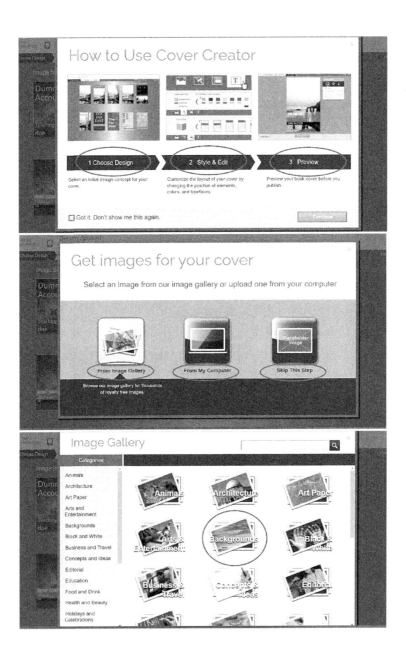

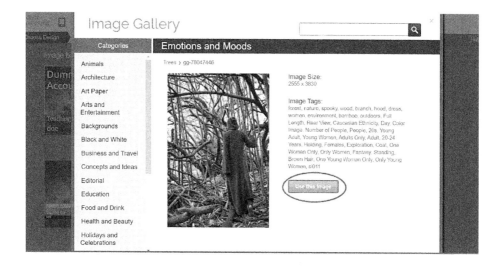

Once you choose a photo for your cover, KDP uses the information you've entered on the Details page to create an assortment of covers to choose from. Finalize your design and save.

79

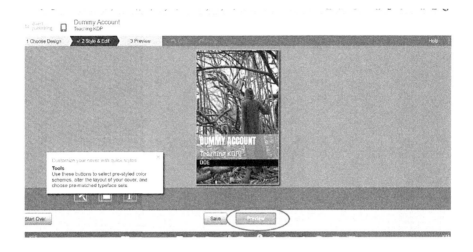

15] At the bottom of the *Content* page, there is a place to *enter an ISBN* if you have purchased one, but ebooks do not need an ISBN, so most people skip this step.

One may also enter the *name of their publisher*. This is not required, but if you have an LLC, I suggest you list your business name if it's on your copyright page.

Again, you can click to *save the draft* for later or, if you're done, click **save and continue** to move to the *Pricing* page.

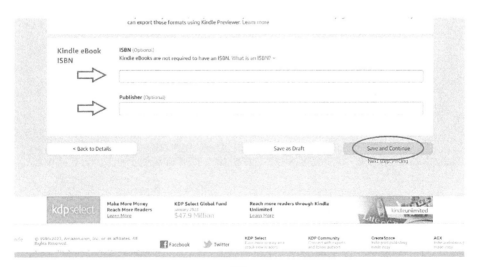

16] On the *Pricing* page, you may click to **enroll your book in KDP Select**, which is also known as Kindle Unlimited to readers. If you select this option, your book must be EXCLUSIVE to Amazon; however, you can be paid for page reads of Kindle Unlimited subscribers. You must weigh whether you make more from other platforms like Kobo, Apple, etc., or Amazon-exclusive page reads. I make more on page reads than I did on Apple and Kobo, so it was worth it for me. And because I run ads in other countries, I get page reads from them, too. You might start broad and see how it goes first.

17] Next, click ***"All territories"*** to sell your book everywhere.

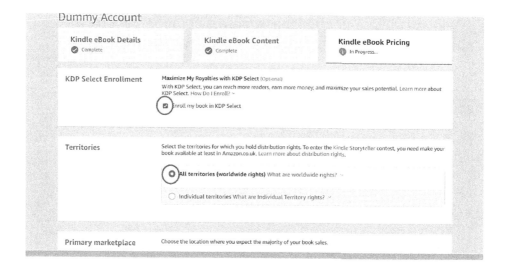

18] If you live in the U.S., your primary marketplace is Amazon.com. **Click this option**.

19] **Set your price**. You can either make 35% of your sales or 70%. You make 70% by pricing your book between $2.99 and $9.99. If you are priced outside that range, you will only make 35% of your sales.

If you try to enter a higher or lower number, the box will turn red (below), so you will have to click on the 35% bubble.

Be careful, though; if you have been at 35% and move your price into the 70% range, you must remember to click the 70% bubble because KDP will happily pay you 35% until you remember to click the bubble. I did this and kicked myself.

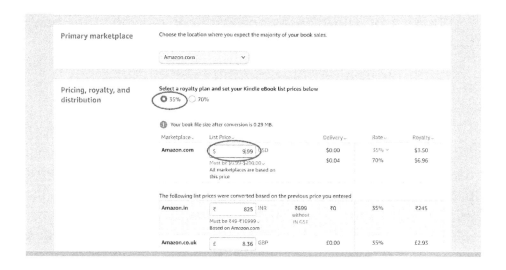

KDP will automatically fill in the prices for the other marketplaces.

20] When you are finished, you can either *save it as a draft* or click the *"Publish"* button. If you have set a preorder date, pressing the *publish* button will begin your *preorder.* If you have not opted for preorder, this will immediately publish your book, and it will appear in the next 72 hours. Note: There is no stopping this. If you click publish, it is a done deal, so be careful.

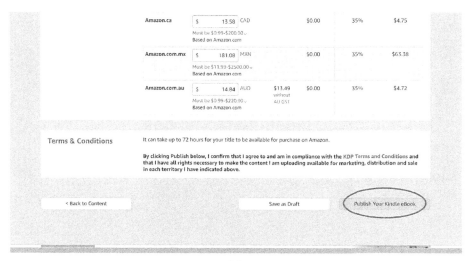

That's it for uploading your ebook. Keep reading to see how to upload your paperback.

Uploading Your Paperback to KDP

When you follow the prompts or click the button on your dashboard to upload your paperback copy, you will go to three pages again: *Details, Content*, and *Pricing*. You will notice that the *details* from your ebook will automatically appear on your paperback's details page. Let's take a look at the paperback pages.

1] First, on the *Details* page, you will double-check your **language**.

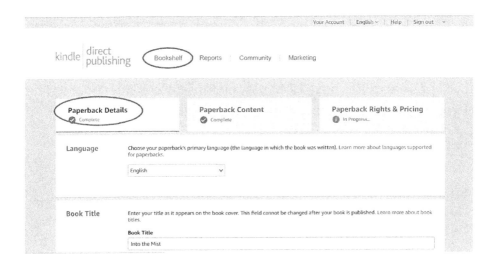

2] Check *title* and *subtitle*. Then make sure your *series* information is correct.

If you desire to use your book as the first book in your series (you can do this with the ebook, if you wish, and the information will already be here), click the button that says, *"**Add series details**,"* and the following box will appear.

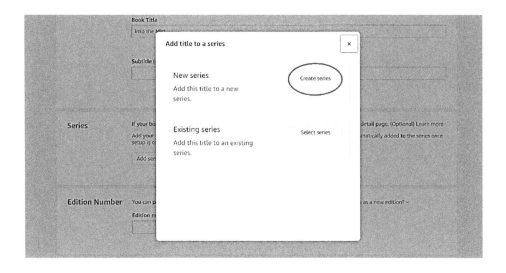

Next to *"New series,"* click the box that says *"**Create series.**"* A new box will appear.

Unless your book is a prequel, short story, or other related content, and is indeed the first book in your series, click *"Main content."*

Follow the prompts to set up your *series page*. This will create a page, especially for this series. Eventually, you can direct readers to this page to see the whole series together, which is less complicated than sending them to your author page if you have more books than that series. Let's go back to the *Details* page.

3] Double-check your **author name**, **contributors**, and **description**.

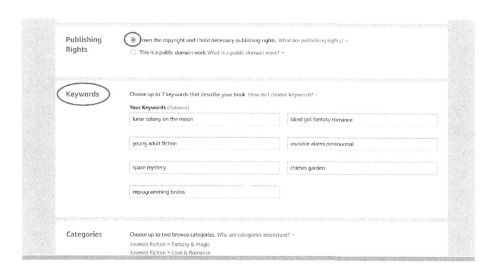

4] Click the bubble next to **"I own the copyright and hold necessary publishing rights."** Then check your **keywords**.

5] You will need to re-enter your **categories**, "Book" categories are different than your ebook categories (And they rank differently). You will need to either use Publisher Rocket with the

"Books" search or, using the menu on Amazon, look under "Book" categories, not "Kindle eBook."

6] After that, you will be asked if the content is for adults. You don't need to worry about age groups and grades this time. It's a yes or no bubble.

When you are done with the page, either save it as a draft or save it and continue to the Content page.

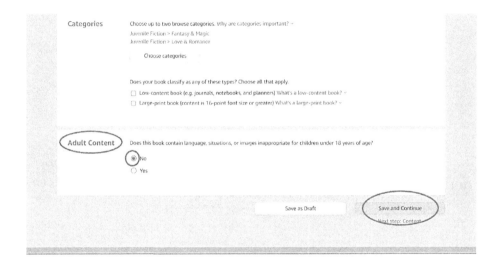

7] On the *Content* page, it will ask you if you'd like them to *assign you an ISBN*. Unless you have purchased ISBNs ahead of time, **click the bubble** for a free one, then **click the yellow box**. You will notice the number appears to the right. Make sure you add this number inside your book on the copyright page. Amazon does check this. (You will get another new ISBN if you create a hardback copy.) Once, I accidentally left my paperback ISBN inside my hardback copy, and KDP emailed me to change it before they would publish the book. So, double-check it.

8] Under that, it says *"Publication date."* Since you are publishing this book for the first time, leave this blank. Amazon will automatically use the day you publish a book for the first time as your publication date. This box is used in case you publish *another* version of your book in the future and you want to retain the original publication date. Otherwise, if you are republishing it, it will show the date of the new edition.

9] Next are your *print options*. **Black and white on cream paper** is for fiction novels, and *black and white on white paper* is generally used for non-fiction books. The slide below show the first print option for ink and paper type.

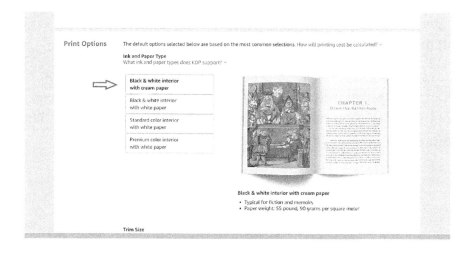

10] Below that is the **trim size**. This is the size of your book. Most paperback novels are 5 x 8" or 5.25 x 8". Many people will make their paperback 5 x 8 and their hardback 6 x 9. These are the two most popular sizes. (Amazon has just increased the price of any books greater than 6 x 9" for the cost of extra paper and ink.)

Bleed settings generally do not apply to most books. A "bleed" setting means that you have colors or other text that will need to be printed to the edge of the page, outside the margins. If so, this will change the size of your inside pages to make sure there is enough room, but KDP should let you know if it's okay in the *print previewer*. Bleed settings are required to be uploaded in pdf form. For most books, you will keep everything inside the margins and will **select "no bleed."**

The *paperback cover finish* will determine if your cover will be **matte or glossy**. This is somewhat a matter of taste; however, you can also check the covers of your comp books and/or choose the feel that you best enjoy on the books you read. Glossy covers are smooth, shiny, and reflective, and the colors can be more vibrant, which is good for highlighting detailed cover art. While matte covers are not shiny or reflective, the colors are slightly muted, and they have a silky texture to the touch. (I have found that my matte covers show fingerprints and smudges more easily, but this is argued among authors.)

Since the cover finish is one of the few things you can still change after publication, you can always order proof copies of both finishes and decide which one works better for your book before you publish it.

For your trim size, you may also click *"Select a different size."* The following slide shows the box that will appear with the available trim sizes.

11] Now, you will ***upload your paperback copy***. PDF is the best format, but you can also upload it in a Word document.

12] Next, for the cover, you will have the same options as the ebook: ***upload your own cover*** or ***use the Cover Creator***. Again, all you need to do is follow the prompts. If you are making your own cover, use your ebook cover as the front cover, and use the same size for your back cover, making sure to leave space for the bar code in the lower right corner. *The size of the spine width will depend on how many pages your book has.*

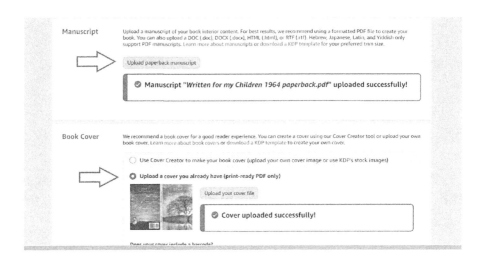

To make it easier, you can go to: https://kdp.amazon.com/en_US/cover-templates and enter your book's details, and it will give you a perfect template for your book cover (below). Notice it tells you the exact sizes. I make my covers in Word, and I take the measurements from the template and make the "document" that size, then I download the template and insert it into the "document" in the correct size. From there, you can easily lay your front cover on the right side of the spine and back cover on the left side of the spine, and then I *"insert shape"* of a rectangle over the spine area and add my text to it. From Word, you can easily *"export"* the cover and create a pdf copy that will upload to your *Content* page perfectly.

[*Update: When you upload your paperback cover, there is a little box that says, *"Check this box if the cover you're uploading includes a barcode. If you don't check the box, we'll add a barcode for you."* This causes some confusion. If you do NOT have a barcode, which is most of us, leave the box blank so Amazon will add the barcode for you in the space you've left for it. ONLY check the box if you already have a barcode.]

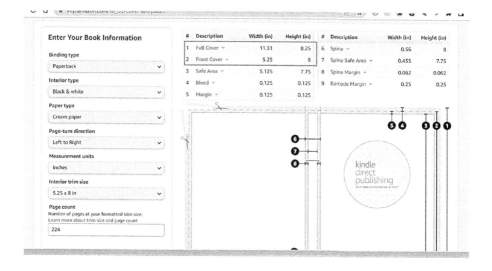

13] At the bottom of the *Content* page is the **book previewer**. Always click this button if you've made changes to your manuscript and/or cover. (If you re-edit your book, or decide it needs changes, simply come back to this page and upload the new copy. But it will only be live after you go through the *Pricing* page and hit "publish.")

When you click the button to launch the previewer, don't worry when it takes a long time to load. It isn't broken. Your book is fine. Occasionally, it goes pretty quickly, but usually, you will see the following screens and maybe more.

You may see the following screen if your laptop has a standard-sized screen, but it's not a big deal. Just click "continue."

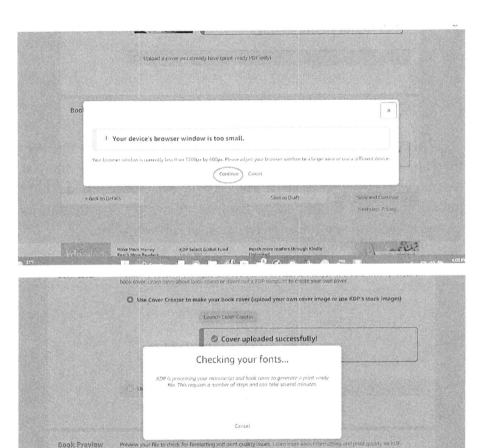

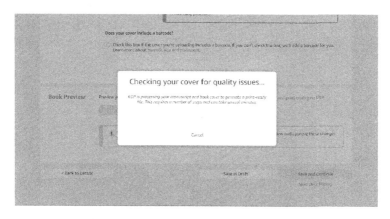

When the previewer finally loads, you will see your cover first. If there are any issues with the cover or the manuscript, or margins, it will tell you what is wrong and what the correct measurements are *in this box*. If there are errors with either the

95

cover or the text, you will have to fix them and re-upload before KDP will accept the book.

Use the arrows to click through your book. Make sure everything looks the way you want it to. Always check your front and back matter carefully. If everything is to your satisfaction, and KDP is okay with your entry, the *"Approve"* button will turn yellow, and you may click it to move on.

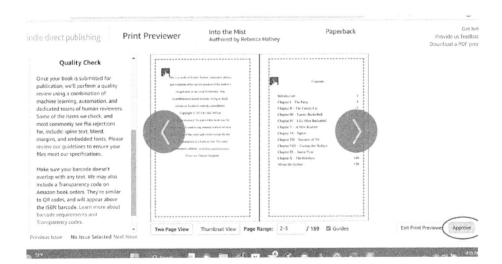

14] You will be taken back to the *Content* page. At the bottom of the page, a *summary* will appear, listing your print details and your printing cost. This is what it will cost you to print the book and buy author copies. (I will explain in the next few pages.)

When you are finished uploading your content, and everything is satisfactory, you may *save it as a draft* or **save it and continue** to the *Pricing* page.

15] On the *Pricing* page, click the first bubble to indicate that you want to **sell your book worldwide.**

16] Again, your primary marketplace in the U.S. is Amazon.com.

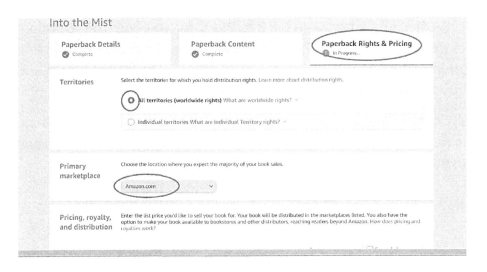

17] Next up is the *Pricing, royalties, and distribution* section. You will earn 40% of your paperback sales, and you may choose your price. However, depending on the amount of your printing costs, KDP will have a minimum and maximum amount that you can charge. If you are below their suggested minimum, the box will be red as follows.

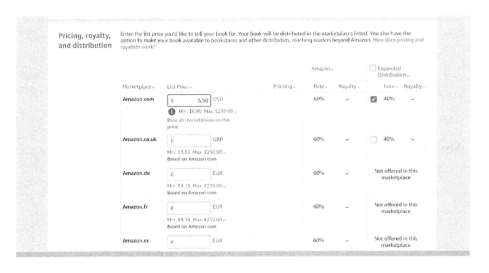

When you enter a satisfactory number, the boxes will fill in and show you what your royalties will be. In this case, our printing cost is $2.76, and our sale price is $6.99. The way that KDP calculates your royalty is by taking your sale price ($6.99) and figuring your percentage (40% of $6.99 =$2.79), and then subtracting your printing costs from that ($2.79 - $2.76 =$0.03), so you will earn $0.03 per paperback sold.

(This is the cheap, miserly way to calculate royalties. If KDP took your sales price, minus your print cost, and *then* figured the percentage, it would be $6.99 - $2.76 =$4.23 x 40% = $1.69, which is a whole lot more than three cents.) As you can see by the following slide, they do allow me $0.04 per copy, but that's not any better, in my opinion. It can be very frustrating.

Pricing, royalty, and distribution Enter the list price you'd like to sell your book for. Your book will be distributed in the marketplaces listed. You also have the option to make your book available to bookstores and other distributors, reaching readers beyond Amazon. How does pricing and royalties work?

Marketplace	List Price		Printing	Rate	Royalty	Expanded Distribution	
				Amazon		Rate	Royalty
Amazon.com	$ 6.99 USD Min. $6.90, Max. $250.00. Base all marketplaces on this price		$2.76	60%	$1.44	☑ 40%	$0.04
Amazon.co.uk	£ 5.85 GBP Min. £3.82, Max. £250.00. Based on Amazon.com		£2.29	60%	£1.22	☐ 40%	£0.05
Amazon.de	€ 6.60 EUR Min. €4.18, Max. €250.00. Based on Amazon.com	€7.06 incl. DE VAT	€2.51	60%	€1.45	Not offered in this marketplace	
Amazon.fr	€ 6.60 EUR Min. €4.18, Max. €250.00. Based on Amazon.com	€6.96 incl. FR VAT	€2.51	60%	€1.45	Not offered in this marketplace	
Amazon.es	€ 6.60 EUR	€6.86 incl. ES	€2.51	60%	€1.45	Not offered in this marketplace	

Note: As of June 20th, 2023, Amazon has raised their cost and will take a greater percentage. So, you must calculate how much you will need to charge to make a profit.

Changes to your printing costs include:

1. *An increase in the fixed cost for all paperback and hardcover books to cover the higher cost of materials, suppliers, and labor.*
2. *A new fixed and per-page cost for paperback and hardcover books with large trim sizes to cover the*

additional costs to print these books. A large trim size is either more than 6.12 inches (155 mm) in width or more than 9 inches (229 mm) in height.

3. *A decrease in the per-page cost for certain color-ink print books ordered from some marketplaces, as shown in the printing cost tables on our Help page.*

In response, Amazon says:

We've created the following tools and information to help you evaluate the impact of the new printing costs on your royalty earnings:

- *See new printing costs and answers to frequently asked questions.*
- *Visit the Pricing tab for each of your live print books to compare your minimum list price, printing costs, and royalty amount by marketplace both before and after the printing costs change.*
- *Visit your KDP Bookshelf to run a one-time bulk list price update on all of your live paperback list prices to continue earning the same royalties after printing costs change.*

18] Under *pricing*, you are given the option to **order proof copies**. These are at author cost, which is your printing cost, *plus* shipping (Even if you have Prime, you will pay shipping for your books.) The book will be printed with a bar across the cover saying it's a *proof copy*. These are good to give out as ARCs (advanced reader copies) to early readers/reviewers. Reviewers often give more grace to books that aren't published yet and assume any mistakes they find will be fixed before publishing. Though, if they find many, they may remark about it in their review, so be careful who you send those to.

When you click this button, the following box appears. Enter the *number of copies* you want and the *marketplace you are ordering from*, and click ***"Submit proof request."*** You may be directed to your cart in Amazon in a new tab to complete the purchase. Then, after making the purchase, you must make sure to go back to the pricing page and move on to #19.

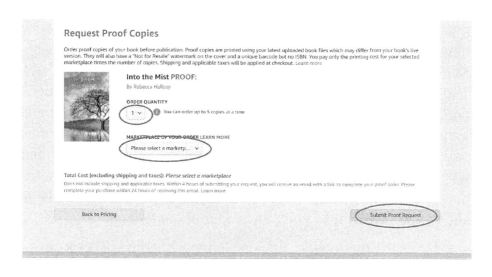

19] When you are finished, return to this page. If you have ordered proof copies and you aren't finished or ready to publish, or if your ebook is on preorder and you want to wait for its launch to publish, make sure to click *"Save as draft"* because once you click *"Publish your paperback book"* your paperback will go live within the next 72 hours, and there's no way to stop it.

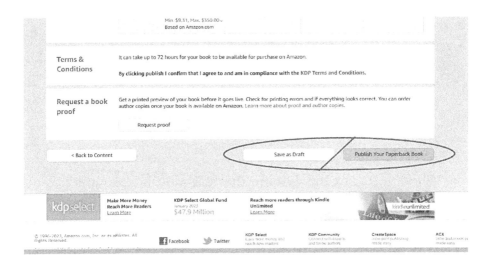

Now, if you pressed it by accident, it's not the end of the world. Your paperback and your ebook/preorder are not connected. Your paperback sales will not "count toward your preorder." Because there is no "preorder" where sales are stored up for launch. Amazon counts each sale as they're made during your preorder. The benefit of publishing your paperback early is that ebook preorders cannot receive reviews; however, paperbacks can, and they share with your ebook page. This is how you will sometimes see a preorder with reviews. It's something I would suggest and will help Amazon see that you are relevant if you make sales during that time, whether ebook or paperback. That could be a secret you give only to your newsletter or something.

That's it. You're done. You can leave a paperback book saved as a *draft* for as long as you want. It's up to you whether you want to wait and launch your different versions at the same time. After you publish your paperback, you will be prompted to upload a *hardback copy.* You can do this at any time. The cover margins will be different, even if you make them the same size, because the cover must be able to wrap around the edges of the book. The covers are printed directly onto the hardback. So, I just make a new blank page in Word, increase my paper size to my hardback size, center my cover, and fill the space to the edge to upload for my hardback.

WHAT ELSE KDP HAS TO OFFER:

Look at the menu above your three pages in KDP. If we click *"Bookshelf"* we will go back to the very first page and see our book listed. But if we click ***"Reports,"*** we go to a whole new page. (You can click *reports* from any page.)

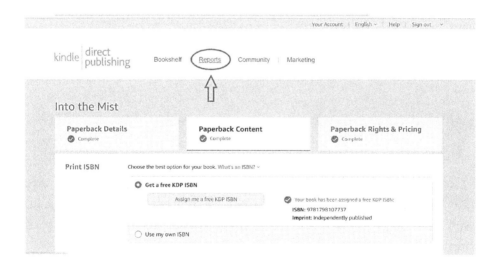

You will also have a Reports Dashboard that shows you this day's royalties, orders, and KENP reads, which are the page reads you have earned through Kindle Unlimited. These are not necessarily the same number of pages as in your book. There is a way to discover how many "pages" KENP allots to your book, so you can divide by your total and see how many full books have been read. (We will find this coming up.)

If you are running Amazon ads in other countries (I advertise in America, Canada, Australia, Germany, and the U.K.), it will show you what percentage of your sales come from which marketplace. That's a lot of fun.

There is a listed menu to the left that will show you various reports.

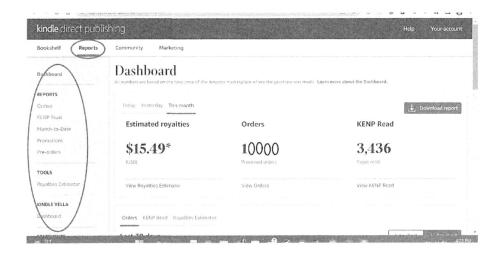

If we go back to the menu at the top, let's click on *"Community."* This opens up the *KDP Community* where you can find answers to most publishing questions you can think up with lots of problems and solutions. There are announcements and forums, and from here, you can get to KDP University, which has a library of videos on how to navigate KDP as well.

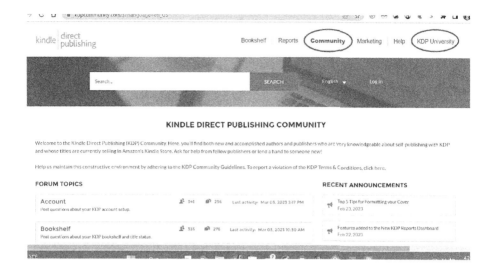

Now, let's go back to the menu and click *"Marketing."* This is an especially important page, and you need to know what is offered here. First, you will find a button where you can decide if you want to enroll in KDP Select. We talked about this earlier. It is called Kindle Unlimited to the readers. If you enroll your book, you will be able to amass page reads by people who have subscribed to Kindle Unlimited, but you must be selling exclusively on Amazon.

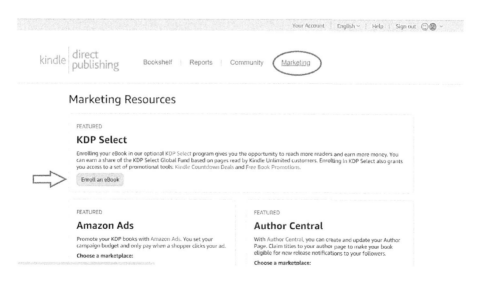

A little further down, you can choose to run ***Amazon ads*** and choose which marketplace (country) you'd like to run your ads. I run constant, low-cost-per-click ads on several Amazon marketplaces. There are many classes and videos that talk about how to do this and make a profit. The good thing is you will discover A] how many times a person sees your ad, B] how many times they click on it, and C] how many times they order. You can target keywords that you want your ad to show up for, or you can target comp books for your ad to show up on their page, so readers of your genre will see you. This can be greatly beneficial. Next to it is where you get to ***Author Central***.

A DEEP DIVE INTO "AUTHOR CENTRAL"

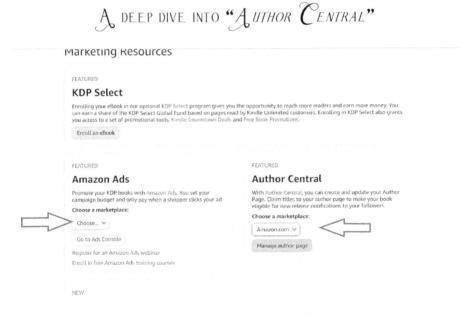

You will need to click on your marketplace (*Amazon.com* for Americans), then click ***"Manage author page."*** You will be directed to a new page that looks like this. You will see *a new menu* at the top, and these are not the same pages as before. We will take a look at each. The first page will say *"Hello"* and give you several options. If you write under more than one pen name, you can click on the upper right-hand corner and toggle between your author pages.

We are going to click on *"View all books"* in just a moment, but first, let's scroll all the way to the bottom of the page. While you are in *Author Central*, the bottom of each page has a menu. *If you ever need to contact KDP about your book* (like when I said to add your seven extra categories), *this is how to find them*. Click ***"Contact us."***

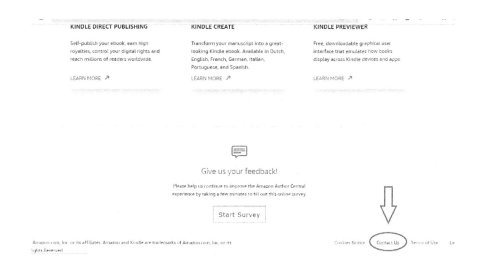

107

The following screen will appear. From the menu on the left, choose what you need help with. In the previous case, we wanted to add categories, so we would click *"Amazon book page"* and then ***"Update Amazon categories."***

The page changes to look like this. You will follow the directions as instructed. For categories, you would fill in any you want removed and any you want added and submit. It will tell you, as it does in this box, what information they require.

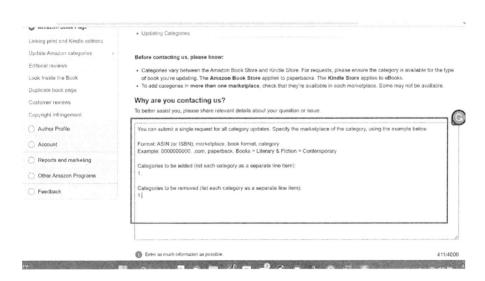

Sometimes you will be required to leave an email, in which you will have to wait about 24 hours to hear back (in the email you use for Amazon). For other issues, you may be asked how you'd like to contact KDP with an option for email or phone. If you click "phone" they will call you with the next available operator.

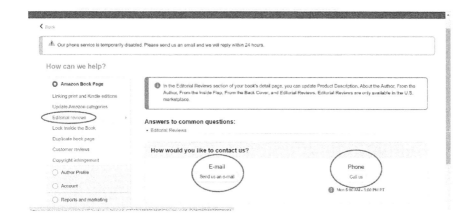

Okay, let's go back to the *Author Central "Home"* page and click ***"View all books."*** Your list of books will appear.

When you click on a cover, it will show you a page with each version of that book. Your choices are *Kindle, Paperback*, and

Hardcover. I always **click on Kindle**, because when a reader looks up your book, they are automatically taken to your Kindle page, so I make sure it's the one I work on. Don't forget to repeat your work for the other formats if it doesn't automatically transfer, but it usually does.

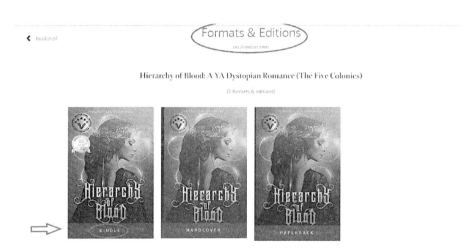

When you see this page, click *"Edit book details."*

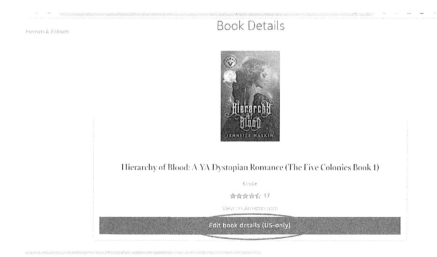

You will be taken to a page where you can enter your editorial reviews. These are reviews by publications and important reviewers who do not leave Amazon reviews. I keep a copy of all my reviews in a file, and if/when Amazon removes my reviews out of nowhere, I add them to my editorial reviews. Once you publish, you will want to get ten reviews as quickly as possible. Most readers like seeing at least ten reviews when choosing a new, untested book.

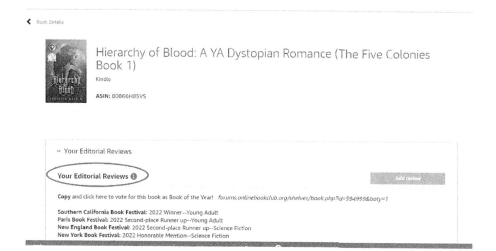

You can also change your *product (Book) description* here, but if/when you happen to change something in your KDP pages and hit "publish," again, KDP will publish whatever description you have on your KDP *Details* page from earlier. So, if you do change your description here, make sure you also change it on your *Details* page in KDP.

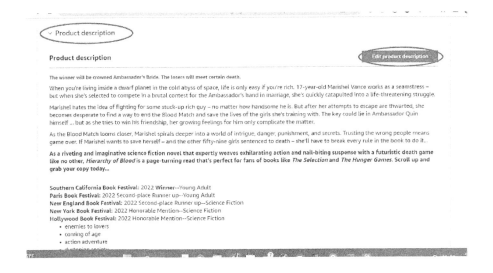

Below that, you can find the place to enter your *"From the Author"* section, *"From the inside flap," "From the back cover,"* and *"About the Author."* These are optional, but you want to at least add your photo and a small bio under *"About the Author"* to go on your sales page, and this will also create your *"Author Page"* on Amazon, where a reader can go to see ALL your books and a bit about you.

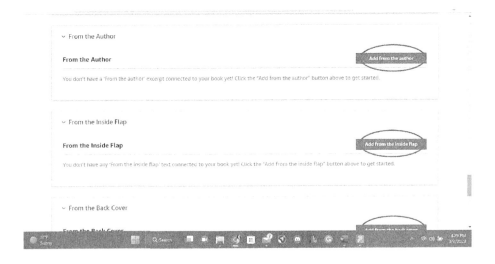

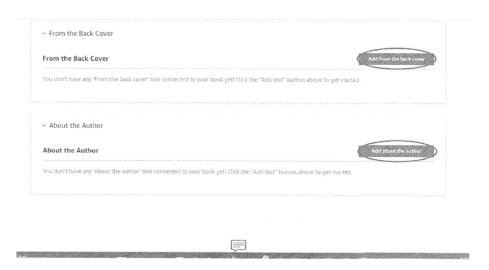

Now that we've seen the *Home* page and your *Books* page, let's click on ***"Reports and Marketing."*** (You can also add book recommendations for your readers here, which is a new service that puts you in the inbox and mind of your readers.)

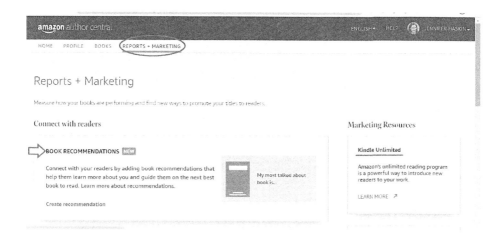

Below that, you can find your ***weekly sales report***, a list of all ***your customer reviews for each book***, and ***your current sales rank***. Let's click on *"Sales rank."* Notice to the right you can also enroll in KDP Select from here, as well as Amazon Advertising.

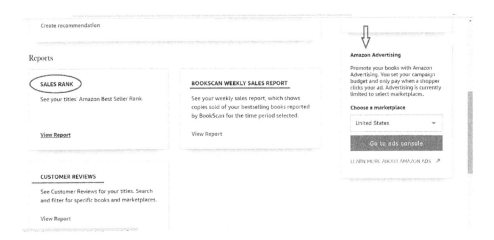

On your *Sales Rank* page, you can select information from different marketplaces, different pen names, and different books. Each entry lists the *current sales rank* for that book, its *historical sales ranking*, the *date you published* the book, and a link to see *your category rankings* on Amazon.

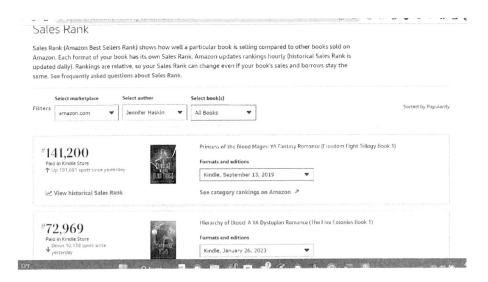

I know this is a lot of information. Bear with me, we're almost done. The good news is that you have this information for the future if you have any questions or don't remember how to find something. For now, let's go all the way back to KDP's original

"Marketing" page. We will scroll down a bit. The next item is called **A+ Content**. You will see this on some sales pages after the description and before the editorial reviews. It says *"From the Editor"* on your page, and you can add images, quotes, and bullet points—just an added bit of pizazz to your page. Simply choose your marketplace and follow the prompts to manage your *A+ Content*. I suggest you look at some of your comp books first to see if they have *A+ Content* and, if so, what they look like before you create yours.

Under that is where you can **run a price promotion** like a *Kindle Countdown Deal*, or a *Free Book Promotion* (You are limited to 5 days of each 90-day enrollment period).

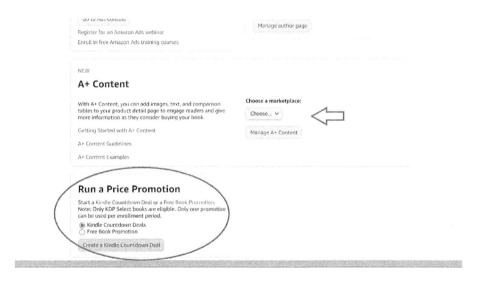

When you click *"Free book promotion,"* a box appears with your books and will let you know which books are eligible for the promotion and allows you to choose your promotion dates.

Next, scroll down the page a little more until you see *"Nominate your ebooks."* This is a nomination for *Kindle Deals* and *Prime Reading Promotions*. You can nominate your book for a period of time and choose to make the nomination reoccur when the time limit lapses.

Under that are more marketing resources and a place where you can buy gift copies of your books to give to people. If you buy a handful and give them to reviewers, their review will be listed as a "verified" review, which holds more weight with Amazon than non-verified reviews. However, I have heard of Amazon removing reviews from gift links because they assume the reviews are biased, so beware.

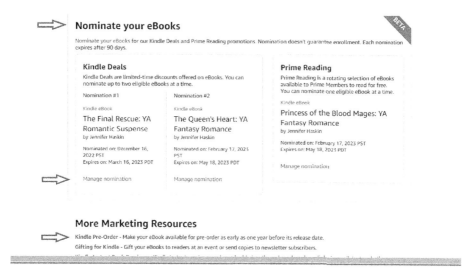

Almost done, I promise. Lol. Finally, let's go to the very top of the page and click *"Your Account."* There is a menu on the side that will show you your *profile information* as an author, a place to *enter your bank information* so you can get paid, *your tax information*, and *your account ID.*

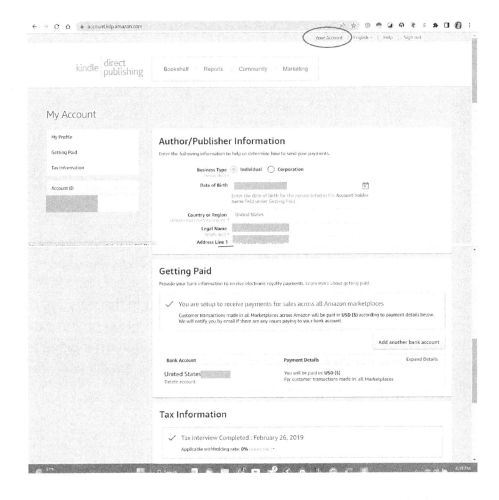

That's it. **_You've done it_**. If you followed along with the text, you have uploaded your book to KDP, and you are ready to publish. If you read through the material first, now it's time to go back and do the work.

1] It will take you some time to find the most lucrative keywords and narrow them down to the best seven, and it will take a couple of hours to make a list of every possible category your book fits in and then decide on the best three.

2] Designing the best description will require you to make a few options to pick the best one or to hire someone with experience in marketable description writing (Don't forget to try Kindlepreneur's AI description generator).

3] You will need to format your manuscripts. Hint: I always write and edit in the ebook format until I am satisfied with its completion, and format it for publishing *before* I create and format the paperback because paperback formatting is more complicated, and if you need to make any more edits, you will have to repeat them in both formats because it isn't an easy copy and paste situation once you're done formatting.

4] You will need to find a cover artist or make your own cover but do *not* skimp on this. **Your cover is your number one tool for marketing.** *Why?* Because when the reader is scrolling through a sea of thumbnail book covers, looking for something to read, it will be your cover alone that attracts them to stop scrolling and be curious enough to click and see what it is. Then, that description will make or lose you the sale, so don't rush through that, either. Remember to focus on the characters and their stakes to excite the reader and create questions they want to be answered or just give them a need to read your story.

5] Finally, upload, and you're done.

6] Once you have followed these instructions, you will move to marketing and promotion. Amazon KDP has options on the Marketing page to help you, and I will eventually make a book on marketing as well.

7] For promotions, I bought a two-year calendar with months only. Whenever I run a promotion, I write it on my calendar and then check my reports page to see if the promotion increased sales on the day(s) it ran and by how much, and since I run ads, I can record my daily impressions, clicks, and sales to see which promotions are the most effective.

This strategy is great for finding the 20% of work that gives 80% results. If you need more information, I have many more files and articles on my blog (www.jenniferhaskin.com) that talk about marketing as well.

The other thing you will hear over and over as you learn marketing is that *the next best piece of marketing is another book*. It's true. When you release a new book, it only **helps** the previous books. You will find, if you're writing a series, that you are constantly *pushing the first book*–especially if they must be read in order. If they can be read in any order, you'll have an easier time marketing them separately. But don't despair. If your readers love the first book, they will likely continue to see what happens. I always pimp the first book in my trilogy because the books must be read in order to make sense. Unfortunately, I see fewer sales than if I marketed all my books, but I don't want to confuse the readers. It's up to you, though. If your series can be read in any order, you have the best of both worlds and can promote any and all of your books at the same time.

Keep in mind if you don't have a great book, nothing you do will help sell the rest of your series. It might get your first book bought, but it won't get you repeat customers. Leading readers to your book is a marketing art form; getting them to buy is a formula, but once they get there, make sure you have a book that will knock their socks off. Make *sure* it is edited.

If you are indie and you spent the last year learning about writing and editing, and marketing, you can easily go back, re-edit your book(s), and publish a "new edition," or just upload the renewed manuscript for the edition you are on. It's simple. Once you've re-edited, go to your *Content* page, where you uploaded your manuscript the first time, and upload the new version, then hit *Publish*. Note: changes will not take effect until you click "publish." You could re-edit it every year if you wanted to. If it makes readers happy, you'll have success.

Good luck self-publishing the "write" way!

A Final Message/Side Note

[Added 1/25/2024]

Since publishing this book, I have had several authors ask me the same question in a variety of ways, saying something like this:

> *Mrs. Haskin, I read your book" Self-Publishing on KDP the Write Way," and I was thinking about uploading a manuscript to KDP. As a first-time author, I am hesitant to do this. I was wondering if you would be interested or available to help me with editing and uploading my book for a reasonable price?*

I received a new request the other day and I thought I would add this side note to help everyone out. First of all, thank you for asking and giving me the opportunity to work with you all. I can edit if my calendar allows. About your anxiety over uploading, I have a suggestion.

Most first-time indie publishers are, at the very least, hesitant about the act of publishing on KDP's site. They assume that as soon as you log in, you will go directly to a page that asks for all your information NOW, and you aren't quite sure you have what you need, but you're sure that if you enter any information and then try to leave the site, you'll probably end up screwing it all up and publishing some trash copy, and it will be forever stuck that way, with your name and picture... Just kidding, mostly.

Know this—and I've said it a million times, but no author listens—***you can get on the site and look around all you like without publishing a thing. You can enter some information if you'd like and click to "save as draft" or "exit without saving," but you don't have to know everything to begin. And nothing is permanent yet.***

Now, once you begin to enter information on the Details page, and you want to "Save and continue" to the Content page, it may require that you fill in additional boxes to continue. Again, do not worry. For all that it matters, you could put *Watermelon* in every box and save it as a draft for now. You can come back to change it as many times as you'd like until the book is published. Even then, some things—like categories, keywords, and descriptions—can still be changed limitless times after that.

Again, *don't worry*. You can't mess this up unless you get to the end and press the button that says, "*Publish*." (KDP staff will review the book before going live and *should* catch it if this happens by mistake.) But don't do that yet, and you'll be fine. I suggest that you log on as soon as possible and get familiar with the site well before you have to upload.

Why do I think this is wise? Because something always goes wrong at the last minute. Or you press publish and notice a problem, etc. UNLESS you log on early, upload the latest copy of your manuscript, and fix any issues beforehand.

KDP's ebook page format is the same as the default page settings in Word, so you should be able to see your book in the "print previewer" without any problems, even if you haven't formatted it yet. This is a great time to look at your cover, too, and see how it all works together, see if the chapters end in the right places, see if KDP finds an error in your book, or make up a cover with the Kindle Create program (I do NOT advise this—see my chapter on Covers), or use it to make a placeholder before your cover reveal.

Once you publish your book, if you come back to these KDP pages and make any changes to your book details or your cover, or you re-edit your manuscript and upload a new copy (which you can do whenever you want ad infinitum), or if you change your price for a sale, even though you may click "Save and exit," nothing will actually change until you click the "Publish" button and submit it again. So don't be afraid that you're going to change something and accidentally publish the wrong edition or save a misspelling or whatever. You can work with it until you're comfortable, and nothing is permanent until you hit "Publish."

If you've found my book helpful, I would log on to KDP as it says in the beginning and follow along to familiarize yourself with the pages— or you may choose to begin entering information—when you have some time, and you are relaxed (Before you begin to enter information, you can click through the three pages as long as you don't save anything yet).

Maybe jot some notes for yourself in your book or download the worksheets and write on those*. Just knowing what you're doing, seeing how simple it is, being comfortable, working through issues early, and doing things at your own pace will help tremendously.

If I were to help you publish—especially for a fee—I would become your traditional publisher. At this time, I don't want to be responsible for anyone else's book(s) or money. But that's why I wrote this book. As long as you go slowly, one step at a time, this book details the steps I would take if I published your book myself—the most important being your keywords, categories, and book description.

I hope this helps some of you be more comfortable and, ultimately, have more confidence with uploading to KDP.

Happy publishing!

* Worksheets can be downloaded from:
https://drive.google.com/drive/folders/1oL0XZ_44nXcfpbTtUDwjsKy_HaAXeN52?usp=sharing

Worksheets

Part One: Need to Know Before Publishing	
Title	
Subtitle (for Amazon--not printed on cover)	
Description (Use back if necessary)	

	1]	
	2]	
	3]	
Keywords for KDP	4]	
	5]	
	6]	
	7]	
	1]	
Categories	2]	
	3]	
Cover design description (general concepts)		
Possible color combinations		
Title font/Caps/Serif		
Author name font/Caps		
Text colors		

Part Two: Formatting the Book			
Ebook formatting checklist: Using Word (Can use Kindle Create) *Macs are different			
Font: Times New Roman, 12 point			
Make sure **first line** is indented to **5mm**			
Line spacing: single --No extra lines between paragraphs			
Margins are 1" all around (this is the default- so you shouldn't have to change anything)			
For each chapter title, highlight and click **Heading 1** on **Home** me e			
Add front matter--title page 1, copyright 2, dedication 3--Center on page			
Insert table of contents after dedication page(Go to *References* page, click **Table of Contents**, choose table)			
Add back matter--acknowledgments, about the author bio, also by the author			
Add page breaks--at the end of each chapter, place your cursor at end of text and click on **Insert** tab,			
then click **Page Break** (Click to show **paragraph marks** to make this easier)			
No page numbers, headers, or footers			
You may upload the file in Word, Epub, or from Kindle Create			

Paperback formatting checklist:			
Font: Times New Roman, 12 point, single spacing, no lines between paragraphs			
Set **Page Size** to 6" x 9" (Some have their paperback 5.5x8 and their hardback 6x9, it's your choice)			

Set Margins:	Page count	Inside (gutter) margins	Outside margins (top, bottom, and edge)
	24 to 150 pages	0.375 in (9.6 mm)	at least 0.375 in (9.6 mm)
*Go to Layout tab, under *page setup*, go to *margins* tab, *pages, multiple pages*, and click "**mirror margins**," then add your other margins and apply to "**whole document.**"	151 to 300 pages	0.5 in (12.7 mm)	at least 0.375 in (9.6 mm)
	301 to 500 pages	0.625 in (15.9 mm)	at least 0.375 in (9.6 mm)
	501 to 700 pages	0.75 in (19.1 mm)	at least 0.375 in (9.6 mm)
	701 to 828 pages	0.875 in (22.3 mm)	at least 0.375 in (9.6 mm)

For each chapter title, highlight and click **Heading 1** on **Home** me   e
Add **Section** breaks--at the end of each chapter, place your cursor at end of text and click on **Layout** tab,
then click **Breaks,** then click **Next Page** (This goes everywhere your ebook had *Page Breaks*)
Add front matter--title page 1, copyright 2, dedication 3--Center on page
Add back matter--acknowledgments, about the author bio, also by the author
Click **Insert** tab, then click **Page Numbers**, choose *bottom* and *center* of page
Optional: Headers--Click **Insert** tab, click **Header**, choose style and type "Title/Author's last name"
Insert table of contents after dedication page
You may need to insert extra blank pages in the beginning to make sure Chap 1 starts on a **facing** page
Export as a PDF file--click on **File** tab, click **Export**, click **Create PDF** --Upload pdf file to KDP

Part Three: Publishing on KDP	
Make an account on KDP-sign in using your existing Amazon account	
Ebook Upload	
Details Page	
Choose language	English
Enter book title and subtitle	Enter your chosen title and subtitle
Enter Author name	Your name
Contributors (are not your cover designer)	Any co-authors and/or page illustrators
Description	Enter your description
Publishing rights	Check the first one- I own the copyright
Keywords	Enter your 7 keywords
Categories*	Choose 3 of the categories on your list
Age range	Must select if you are writing YA or children's
Pre-order*	Only enter a date if you choose pre-orders
Save and Continue	Or save as draft if you need to make adjustments
Content Page	
Digital Rights Management	Yes--inhibits unauthorized distribution
Upload formatted manuscript	
Upload cover	
Launch previewer	Always view the previewer before accepting
Accept	When satisfied
Save and continue	Or save as draft if you need to make adjustments
Pricing Page	
KDP	Exclusive to Amazon/Gain for page reads
Territories	All territories
Marketplace	Amazon.com
Pricing, royalty, and distribution*	$2.99-$9.99=70%/Less or more than $2.99-$9.99=35%
Book lending	Check--if possible
Save as draft or submit	Beware! If pre-ordering, "submit" sets the date, if not, "submit" publishes the ebook within the next 72 hours.

Part Four: Publishing on KDP (Continued)	
Paperback Upload	
Details Page	
Choose language	English
Enter book title and subtitle	Enter your chosen title and subtitle
Enter Author name	Your name
Contributors are not your cover designer	Any co-authors and/or page illustrators
Description	Enter your description
Publishing rights	Check the first one- I own the copyright
Keywords	Enter your 7 keywords
Categories*	Choose 3 of the categories on your list
Adult content	Is this inappropriate for children? Yes or No?
Save and continue	Or save as draft if you need to make adjustments
Content Page	
Print ISBN	Unless you bought your own ISBN, click to get one
Publication date	Leave blank
Print Options*	B&W/ Cream paper, 6x9, no bleed, glossy cover
Upload formatted manuscript	
Upload cover	
Launch previewer	Always view the previewer before accepting
Accept	When satisfied
Double check summary	
Save and continue	Or save as draft if you need to make adjustments
Rights and Pricing Page	
Territories	All territories
Marketplace	Amazon.com
Pricing, royalty, and distribution*	$2.99-$9.99=70%/Less or more than $2.99-$9.99=35%
Request printed proofs	Suggested
Save as draft or publish paperback*	"Publish your paperback" publishes the paperback edition within the next 72 hours. An ebook on pre-order cannot get reviews, but the paperback copy may get reviews even while the ebook is in pre-order. It will not affect your ebook.

~ Links and Notes page ~

Book Title Generators:

https://writingexercises.co.uk/story-title-generator.php

https://storytoolz.com/generator/half-title

http://www.adazing.com/titles/use.php

Book Description Generator (HTML):

https://kindlepreneur.com/amazon-book-description-generator/

Publisher Rocket Tool -- Jenn's affiliate link:

https://haskinauthor--rocket.thrivecart.com/publisher-rocket/

Amazon Author Central (contact them with your additional categories and anything else you need):

www.AuthorCentral.com

Derek Murphy -- self-publishing guru:

www.Creativeindie.com

Dave Chesson -- tools for self-publishing authors:

www.kindlepreneur.com

Notes:

Worksheets can be downloaded from:

https://drive.google.com/drive/folders/1oL0XZ_44nXcfpbTtUDwjsKy_HaAXeN52?usp=sharing

Jennifer Haskin is passionate about helping new authors with their writing journey and achieving their publishing goals. Eight years ago, she learned the ropes of the publishing world as a literary agent for a boutique agency before moving to a New York-based agency (then had to drop out for a string of back surgeries), then she returned as a publishing consultant, helping authors ready their submission materials to get the best shot at the contract of their dreams. Now, she works as a professional Reedsy editor, Associate Editor for a small press, and head editor of her own business.

Jennifer debuted as a traditionally published author, but she prefers the control of indie publishing. She markets her YA scifi/fantasy/romance fiction novels and non-fiction series "The Journey to a Bestseller" and is always writing a new series. Her website features a blog called "a hidden gold mine of information" for new authors that documents some of her writing journey with weekly advice on writing, editing, publishing, and marketing. She's been on all sides of the publishing business.

Jenn lives in Kansas with her hubsalot and five teenagers, who provide plenty of YA angst to help her writing come alive. When she is not drinking a grande iced white mocha and writing a book or editing manuscripts, she's running a weekly writers' workshop and is honored to be a judge for the annual writing contest Ink & Insights. Come find her on social media and say hi @haskinauthor.

www.jenniferhaskin.com

Don't miss the next book in this series!

Preorder *Launching and Marketing The Write Way* today

And get it November 15th!

www.amazon.com/dp/B0CVQGQ2MK

)

Printed in Great Britain
by Amazon

38729074R00076